I've enjoyed listening to Dan s[ _____ many years. *Authentic Leadership* _____ his message to another level. I highly recommend this book to anyone who wants to build up people and develop better teams, while staying true to themselves.

Brian Miller, President & CEO, ProVia

Dan Owolabi, like most of us, was sure that fitting in mattered. But as a minority in a tradition-steeped community it didn't come easy. The answer—Dan became real. His insights in this book are the same—and they're a real inspiration.

Mark Coblentz, Owner, Walnut Creek Foods

*Authentic Leadership* is for everyone, from CEOs to people on the front lines, who are on a "journey back to the best version of themselves." At the core of sustained organizational long-term success today is Authentic Leadership. We need this type of leadership across our organizations. Dan provides a road map for all of us on this journey. He has a wonderful ability to weave story and practical principles into a very helpful narrative on this powerful concept. I highly recommend this book to people across organizational life.

Jim Smucker, PhD., President of Keim

## LEADERSHIP AUTHORITIES

*Authentic Leadership* is the gold standard for leaders of all ages who want to lead with influence. Dan Owolabi captures the practice of servant leadership with convincing examples and memorable stories. Anyone who takes leadership seriously will significantly benefit from Dan's practical wisdom on authenticity in leadership.

Steve McClatchy, Author of *The New York Times* best-selling book, *Decide*

We need authentic leaders at all levels. In a world where trust, service, and positive relationships are defining characteristics of effective leaders, *Authentic Leadership* is an indispensable book. It's the first stop for anyone who wants to make a lasting difference in the world.

Jon Gordon, Author of *The New York Times*
best-selling book, *The Energy Bus*

## SPIRITUAL AUTHORITIES

Dan Owolabi persuasively writes from a place of expertise and experience on what it truly means to become an Authentic Leader. He not only challenges us to be Authentic Leaders but gives us principles we can use to develop this important element of effective leadership.

Dwight Mason, Lead Pastor, NewPointe Community Church

Much like he speaks, Dan shares a great mix of storytelling, vulnerability and practical wisdom. As a personal friend, I can attest to Dan's introspective look at life and of the pertinent lessons it teaches. He is a solid teacher but even a better student as these pages attest to. The Authentic Leader is a must have resource both for personal growth and to study together with others.

Bruce Hamsher, Founder of Toward the Goal Ministries

We need authentic leaders now more than ever. In *Authentic Leadership*, Dan Owolabi casts a compelling vision for leaders who have nothing to hide, prove, or lose. Every leader should strive to be an authentic leader and this book provides a clear path to becoming one. You will benefit greatly from Dan's story and practice of authentic leadership. Thank you, Dan!

Nick Cleveland, Lead Pastor, Grace Church (Wooster, Ohio)

Dan Owolabi is a dynamic communicator, compelling writer and authentic leader. This book will inspire you with principles and best practices to grow as an authentic leader. This is how we change our world for good and for God.

Larry Kaufman, Lead Pastor, Grace Church (Berlin, Ohio)

# AUTHENTIC
# LEADERSHIP

# AUTHENTIC LEADERSHIP

HOW TO LEAD WITH NOTHING TO HIDE,
NOTHING TO PROVE & NOTHING TO LOSE

## DAN OWOLABI

ISBN (Paperback): 978-1-7350473-0-0
ISBN (e-Book): 978-1-7350473-1-7
ISBN (Audible Book): 978-1-7350473-2-4

Edited by: Emily Krichbaum
Copy Editing and Production by: Catherine Leek of Green Onion
    Publishing
Interior Design by: Kim Monteforte of Kim Monteforte Graphic
    Design Services
Front Cover Design by: Brian Wrensen of Captain Creates

This book is dedicated to the
incredible women in my life.

My daughters, Eden and Anniston.
My mother, Sheila Owolabi.
And above all, my wife, Erica.
You have been a constant source
of inspiration and support.

# CONTENTS

# The Authentic Leader

# Becoming an Authentic Leader

# ACKNOWLEDGEMENTS

I'm deeply grateful to the individuals who have helped make *Authentic Leadership* a reality. I feel humbled that God has surrounded me with a crowd of uniquely talented people. My thoughts are summarized by Albert Einstein when he said, "Every day I remind myself that my inner and outer life are based on the labors of other men, living and dead, and that I must exert myself in order to give in the same measure as I have received and am still receiving." It is true with this book. I could not have written it without the support of many, many people.

Special thanks to Jill Sisson and Brian Miller.

Jill's support fueled every part of this project. Particularly her initial insistence that I write it, and her ability to keep the book on schedule. Without her support, patience, and creativity we'd still be talking about this book instead of reading it.

Brian's presence in my life has been an unending source of support and encouragement. For years, his generosity and wisdom has inspired me to take on greater challenges. I'm grateful to Brian for many, many good things in my life.

Also thanks to:

Ty Hamsher, for his patience and encouragement as we traveled around the world with Branches Worldwide.

Particularly for his understanding as I wrote *Authentic Leadership* in a coffee shop in Thailand, and on a beach in Jamaica.

Jalaine Mast, for her enthusiasm and energy during the slow seasons of this project. I'm extremely thankful she joined Owolabi Leadership.

Terry Shue, for his constant inspiration and support. He's been nothing short of a second father, and I'm forever grateful.

The Board Members of Branches Worldwide, including Steve Tybor, Jill Taylor, Brenda Miller, Nick Cleveland, Eddie Steiner and Anthony Kaufman. *Authentic Leadership* was written during a critical time in the growth of Branches Worldwide, and their open minded flexibility has allowed me to complete it.

Chris White, for his ideas, suggestions, and advice on improving the manuscript.

Jane Atkinson, for her guidance and expert advice as I began the writing process.

Jim and Glenda Snavely, for opening their home on Lake Cable, and allowing me to write by the waves.

My sister Elizabeth and my brother Sam, for holding me accountable to practice what I preach. There's no way they would let me write a book that I didn't live out on a daily basis.

My mother-in-law, Gloria Mishler, for offering excellent edits and corrections in the final stages of this book.

Our editor Emily Krichbaum, for helping develop the structure and tone of the book. Without your initial and extended input, this book would not have the flavor it does.

Ken Hostetler and Marshall Baird, for years of encouragement, input, and conversation that generated great ideas.

Tyler Barney, for inspiring me to put my best work into this book, for the sake of the incredible leaders who will come behind me.

To our many clients, who have provided an ongoing laboratory to apply and validate the Authentic Leadership approach, including Keim Lumber, The University of Findlay ProVia, and ForeverLawn.

With deep gratitude I acknowledge my parents, Tim and Sheila Owolabi. Their courageous journey from Nigeria to the United States overcame stereotypes, defied all odds, blazed the trail, and has provided a source of perpetual inspiration. They made the most of the talent God gave them, and I am forever grateful.

Most of all, I thank God for his presence in my life. He is the leader of my life in the forgiver of my sins, and for that I am grateful beyond measure.

# Great Leaders Are Like Great Runners

"Leaders aren't born, they are made.
And they are made just like anything
else, through hard work."

VINCE LOMBARDI

In 2013 I ran a half marathon. It was my first one. Not just my first half marathon, but my first race *ever*. I'd always wanted to finish one, and I was pretty confident I was going to kill it. I mean, I thought I was going to run *circles* around people. As a former college athlete, I'd been around athletics my whole life, and I thought "C'mon, it's only 13.1 miles. How hard can it be?"

Originally, the idea to sign up for the race came from my wife, Erica. She had decided to run, and she trained the right way. She planned her workouts months in advance. She built up stamina by running daily after work. She ran with her family and friends for accountability. After watching her for a while, I decided I wanted to do it too. But I didn't need *nearly* as much training as she did.

With only three weeks to race day, I created a quick training plan and got started. On day one, I ran 1 mile. On day two, I ran two miles. Day three, three miles, etc. The plan was foolproof—as far as I knew—and still left me with plenty of rest days if I needed. This was going to be great!

When race day arrived, it turned out I took too many rest days. I had only managed to run ten of the thirteen miles. It was a dark, frosty, October morning in Columbus as I lined up with thousands of other runners. The gun went off, and determined to use enthusiasm to make up for my lack of preparation, I started fast and strong, almost sprinting out of the gate.

Right away I passed people left and right, feeling confident, and thinking "Holy crap! I'm much, *much* better than I realized."

After the fifth mile, I started to slow down a bit, but I kept a brisk pace. I saw some runners stop for energy packs or Gatorade. Not me. I was on a mission!

Then, in the middle of mile six, the pain hit me. Gradually at first, then all at once. It started in my lungs, then pushed down towards my legs, and finally exploded out of my toes. By mile eleven, I was a limping, sweaty, groaning mess, barely putting one foot in front of the other. Astonishingly, I still thought things were going okay. Not as well as I had hoped, but hey, at least I was still moving.

The moment of reckoning came in mile twelve. My back was arched, my mouth was dry, and I think I was heaving. I looked over just in time to see a short, pudgy, middle-aged woman passing me on my right. She was wearing a fanny pack. She confidently blurred past me, moving at least twice as fast as I was.

But she wasn't even running. She was *power walking!*

That's the moment I knew I was done. I didn't care that I was less than a mile from the finish line, or that there were hundreds of spectators watching me. The only thing I cared about was stopping the pain. I was unprepared. I was excruciatingly tired. I was *done*!

What's worse? The tired snuck up on me. It was as if the feeling of exhaustion was multiplied by my lack of preparation for it.

Leadership is a lot like that race. Most people who start a business or get a promotion or lead for the first time have a decent grasp of what the actual work of leadership looks like. But what hits them out of nowhere is the pervasive sense of insecurity. It's hard to shake. The feeling that you're not enough. The sense that you suddenly have something to hide, something to prove, or something to lose.

Leaders feel insecurity like distance runners feel tired. It's not a question of *if* runners will feel tired, but *when*. They know the tired is coming—there's no doubt about it. But when the tired comes, the best runners have a plan for it. They've invested months of physical and mental training in preparation for the exact moment when exhaustion hits. The best leaders are no different. They know insecurity is in their future. They don't like it, and they'd rather avoid it, but they're always prepared for it.

I wrote *Authentic Leadership* to give you bad news and good news. Here's the bad news: if you want to lead anything worthwhile, acute moments of insecurity are in your future. You *will* feel anxious, uncertain, and doubtful about your ability to lead. There's no way around it. But here's the good news: authenticity is a potent antidote to insecurity. Authentic Leaders are the most confident, resilient leaders because they prepare to lead every day with nothing to hide, nothing to prove, and nothing to lose.

# PART ONE

# The Insecure Leader

# CHAPTER 1

# When Insecurity Strikes

"The privilege of a lifetime is to
become who you truly are."

CARL GUSTAV JUNG

Leadership is like being a parent. Before the baby comes, you
can't help but dream of how much fun it'll be, how the baby
will naturally connect with you, and how you'll avoid the
eye-rolling mistakes your parents made.

But when the baby arrives and it's your turn to get your
arms around the responsibilities of parenting, you find that
the baby is lactose intolerant, won't stop crying, and doesn't
really like being around you at all! When your experience
doesn't match your expectations, it can be hard to handle.

This is the painful reality for scores of people who become
leaders for the first time, or who take on greater leadership
responsibilities. And the process of coming to terms with

the difficulty of leadership presents a choice: You can lead through authenticity, or you can lead through insecurity. Too often, leaders make the wrong choice.

## The Root of the Problem

Take for example a coaching session I had with an executive a few years ago. It was six o'clock in the morning. One of those mornings that makes you stop, look up, and thank God you're alive. (The exact opposite of how I felt when "Fanny Pack Lady" passed me.) The sun barely shone through the trees—subtly highlighting the various greens of the leaves, grass, and landscape. You don't forget a morning like that. But there was another reason that morning stood out as memorable. I was sitting across the table from a man who was anything but thankful. His life, in short, was a mess. A mess he created and didn't know how to clean up.

We'll call him Tom. He called me the night before in desperation. Normally he was an energetic guy, the kind who was always the biggest guy in the room and never met a stranger. But last night on the phone, his breathing was strained. Between long pauses he stuttered, sobbed, and struggled to speak. He felt dejected, as if he couldn't believe his life had fallen apart so quickly. As we talked, I learned he'd tried almost everything, working later hours, stretching himself thinner and thinner, pulling every lever he had available to him. Nothing worked.

Apparently, I was the last resort.

But I didn't mind. I knew leaders are most capable of bouncing back after they hit the bottom. Tom was clearly at the bottom, and he was a unique case. I told him I'd meet him at six o'clock the next morning at a local coffee house.

When I first met Tom, years before, I thought he looked like a conventional leader. A tall, athletic man in his early forties, he had a touch of gray and a square jaw. As a newly promoted executive in a large Midwest manufacturing firm, he was well positioned for a bright career. At the time, Tom would have considered himself a well-liked person, highly regarded by his peers. Joining the firm over ten years before, Tom believed he knew how to get things done. He spoke in a confident, even tone, invested in a stellar wardrobe, worked long hours, and knew the firm's products from the inside out. Tom considered himself the type of guy you could call on a Thursday night if you had a flat tire. He was friendly with everyone, worked to remember customers kids' names, the CEO's anniversary, the secretary's alma mater. When Tom was tapped for a promotion to the C-suite, he was beyond elated. The new role came with a slate of new responsibilities, a huge platform, and a major bump in salary. It was all an emerging executive could wish for.

Then six months later, all at once, Tom couldn't seem to do anything right. And he cried—in front of me and over his coffee with the sun rising over him.

"First," he explained, "I lost a bunch of deals. It seemed like my key customers just stopped trusting me. Then, two of my most steadfast and trustworthy employees left the firm—and, boy, were they frustrated with me! And to add salt to the wound, they each accepted positions with the rival firm across town."

Tom buried his head in his hands. "Now the CEO is starting to openly question my ability to lead my department!"

His problems didn't end at work. The night he called me, the night before our morning coffee, his wife kicked him out of the house. She was prepared to file for divorce. Initially, I wondered why Tom called me. But as he explained his situation, I understood. Tom simply had no one else. After investing all his energy into his career, he had neglected everything and *everyone* else.

Tom sat slumped in the booth wearing the same shirt—I imagine—from the night before, wrinkled with the top four buttons undone. Tom mumbled under his breath, that he simply didn't know what to do. He emphatically pointed out that he'd tried. He'd tried so hard. Tried to get sales leads. Tried to earn his CEO's trust. Tried to work on his marriage. "I'm trying. I'm trying. I'm trying." He said "Can't. They. See. I'm. *Trying.*"

Suddenly his mind fixated on a new thought. "What if I *can't* turn this around? What if it doesn't matter how hard I try? What if I lose my job? What if my wife goes through with the divorce? What will my parents say? What will my co-workers think? There's no way I could face my friends … oh man, oh man, oh man!"

Tom pounded his fist on the table and pulled at his hair. I listened and held my coffee. Tom was exasperated, and I thought the best medicine was giving him the space to vent. I could see why he was frustrated. As he rehashed his situation, the root problem came into focus.

## Every Leader Battles with Insecurity

Tom's leadership success to this point was an exercise in performance. At home and at work, he was forever trying to demonstrate that he was a leader—to his CEO, his customers, his wife, his friends. It was wreaking havoc on his most critical relationships. This was an acute moment of insecurity, and Tom was not prepared for it.

For starters, Tom didn't consider himself a natural leader, yet for nearly two decades of his life he constantly found himself in leadership positions. He considered each an accident. Tom admitted that he'd desperately wanted to be understood as a capable leader by the people in his life, but each time he experienced significant success he could only question it rather than celebrate it. And when he stumbled, an internal voice told him fate was catching up to him. Everyone would finally see him as a fraud. In his mind, his success was a ticking time bomb. It was only a matter of time until it would end, explode, and crumble.

As I sat with him that morning at the coffee house, I could tell he was beginning to believe time was up. The bomb was going off, and all he could do was clumsily attempt to salvage each blown up part of his previous life.

His wife would leave him, his employees would quit, he'd get fired.

Tom worked overtime to present a confident exterior he hoped would silence his increasingly insecure interior. After sharing morning coffee, it was clear to the both of us that *that* performance wasn't working.

As a pastor, then as a leadership coach, I've worked with a lot of Toms. Different fruit, same root: insecurity.

*No one*, especially leaders, wants to feel insecure. Insecurity, put simply, is a deep feeling of anxiety and uncertainty about yourself. It's the feeling you get when you're doing something difficult or new. Or when you're doing something old and familiar, but the stakes are higher. It's an acute lack of confidence that makes you suspicious, overprotective, self-conscious, and easily offended. Insecurity makes you want to hide your mistakes. It makes you terrified of failure and feel overwhelming anguish when you finally taste it. Sometimes insecurity looks like unnecessary bravado. Sometimes it looks like unexplainable cowardice. Everybody hates insecurity.

> SOMETIMES INSECURITY LOOKS LIKE
> UNNECESSARY BRAVADO; SOMETIMES
> LIKE UNEXPLAINABLE COWARDICE.

If things were perfect, we'd all be humble, salt-of-the-Earth leaders. We'd all have easy, natural confidence, clear vision, and unshakable principles that would guide us through hard times. We'd be known for our consistency, stability, and time-tested skills. We'd never feel the urge to quit, impress others, or be liked. We'd proudly wear our own skin, comfortably resting in our perfection and basking in the glow of people's respect for us.

But leaders are humans, not robots. We make mistakes; we battle insecurities.

For some, this might sound strange. Leaders often seem like the most secure people on earth. They're the ones with the vision, the plan, and the energy to get it done. The men and women who are sure of themselves amid unsure situations. Leaders are not insecure, period. In fact, it it's hard not to think that "leadership" is synonymous with "confidence."

## The Gap

I'm convinced that, behind the scenes, most coaches, bosses, CEOs, and presidents are different than they seem. The most insidious problem that befalls leaders starts with a secretly unaddressed gap. I mean that as a leader, if you could be honest with your team, you might make one of the following confessions:

- I may be in charge, but I don't always know what to do.
- I may be in charge, but I don't have all the answers.
- I may be in charge, but I'm never the smartest person in the room.

That's our little leadership secret, isn't it? This confession makes one uncomfortably aware of a gap that exists between who you are and who people think you are.

- The distance between your performance and your true self.

- The space between the hard reality of who you are and who you wish you were.
- The difference between your real character and your perceived character.

The gap between the *perception* of who you are and who you *really* are is where insecurity thrives. If you've ever felt a persistent feeling of uncertainty, anxiety, and self-doubt, you know how quickly it kills your confidence. You know what an insecurity gap feels like. You may have a wide gap or a narrow gap, but it's the *unaddressed* gaps in your life that cause many of your worst choices.

I was fortunate to be among the seven percent of high school athletes to play sports at the collegiate level. I was on the Malone University basketball team, and when I got to campus my freshman year, I *knew* I was pretty good. And I wanted everyone to know it too. I once carried a basketball to English class, just in case my professor or anyone else in the room wondered if I was bound for basketball greatness. If they weren't sure, the ball under my arm while I read Annie Dillard was a dead giveaway. Mind you, my unshakable self-confidence came before a single practice session.

When the first practice came, I infuriated my teammates by demanding the ball, missing easy shots, and playing lousy defense. Eventually coach got the picture. I was much more sizzle than steak. And after a year of riding the pine and getting dunked on a lot, I began to get the picture too.

At first, I blamed the coach. Then I blamed my teammates. Then I blamed a nagging injury. Finally, I realized I had an insecurity gap. There was a cavernous gap between how good I thought I was, and how good I actually was.

One day after a workout, a caring (and blunt) teammate approached me. The upperclassman (presumably sick of my swagger) put his finger in my chest. He said firmly and quietly, "Dan, if you took the energy you spent trying to *look* like an all-star, and used it to *work* on being an all-star, you'd *actually* be an all-star."

Ouch.

My first thought was, "Who are *you*? What do *you* know?"

In other words, my first reaction was complete and utter defense mode, to shirk back into my shell, protected, not exposed.

I'm not sure how he saw it—maybe everyone saw it—but I vainly attempted to cover it up with excuses and pretense. I pushed his finger off my chest and walked away without saying a word. I was furious. Later that night, as my head hit the pillow, I realized he wasn't wrong. And I needed to hear it.

It takes a tremendous amount of energy to keep up illusions. It's exhausting to maintain the gap between who you are and who you'd like people to think you are. Dave Ramsey agrees. In his book, *The Total Money Makeover*, Ramsey challenged readers to stop living to impress others. He famously said, "We buy things we don't need with money we don't have to impress people we don't like."[1]

Most people are squarely in that boat. We spend far more time, money, and energy looking like we have it together than actually having it together. We clothe the gap instead of closing the gap. So, my question to you is this. What are you pretending? What are you not owning? What do you need to work on?

## What the Heck is Slack-Fill?

If you worked in the packaging industry, you'd be familiar with the term "nonfunctional slack-fill." In fact, you might be so familiar with it that you'd know there's a federal law against it. For the millions of people outside the packaging industry, "slack-fill" is the gap between the bag your chips come in and the chips themselves. Slack-fill is the air in the bag. It's essentially the difference between perception and reality. If a bag contains *functional* slack-fill, then the air in the bag legally serves a packaging purpose. If the air doesn't serve a legitimate purpose and it's designed to trick you into thinking you're getting more chips in each bag, then it's called *nonfunctional* slack-fill.

I wasn't familiar with nonfunctional slack-fill (NSF), but now I thank God there's a law against it. My first and last NSF moment came when I was at the Wal-Mart with my two-year-old daughter. The grocery list was long. My daughter's patience wasn't. While I tried to figure out what exactly tarragon was and where I could find it, my daughter started crying, wailing, gnashing of teeth. You know the scene. The seasoned mothers took pity. Those without progeny looked upon me with disgust. This was my first "Wal-Mart Meltdown" and in a panic I pressed the nuclear button. I went into parental DEFCON 1: bribes.

"Will you zip it if I give you some chocolate?" I said that in my best pastor voice.

Through tears, she smiled and instantly stopped crying.

So, I grabbed the nearest, big bag of chocolate covered pretzels. (I was far, far from the tarragon).

"This bag is full of delicious chocolate pretzels. You can have this whole, big, big bag when we get into the car." Instant smiles the rest of the evening. Dad, the sucker, had lost this round, but at least I got out of Wal-Mart before someone called Child Protective Services.

In the car, away from the judgement and empathic looks of passersby, I pulled out the beautiful bag of saving grace. To my horror, as I opened the bag, I saw a bag full of NSF.

The very full-looking bag was less than half full.

The other half? Air.

My daughter looked at me like I had just killed Curious George. Even Stephen King couldn't have envisioned the next twenty minutes in that car. It was the stuff nightmares are made of.

And, from that nightmare on parking lot row, I now understand why there's a federal law against NSF.

There's a palpable feeling of disgust when encountering the gap between reality and perception. In my research, years ago, I learned that shady manufacturers would hide the actual volume of product they were selling inside a package that looked like it contained twice the amount. People, therefore, would pay more for a lot of fluff. But, as my daughter can attest, you cannot eat fluff.

Federal code states that, "a container that does not allow the consumer to fully view its contents shall be considered to be filled as to be misleading if it contains nonfunctional slack-fill." Essentially, there can't be gaps between the product being purchased and what people think they're getting. If it looks like an authentically full bag of chocolate pretzels, legally it must be a full bag of chocolate pretzels. (I'm looking at you Flipz®!)

Now, there are a handful of good and legal reasons why a company would create a product with functional slack-fill. Sometimes it's necessary to create a gap between the real and the perceived. Manufacturers might insert air to protect the product. Or, air could show up in the product because of settling over time.

> **SOMETIMES IT'S NECESSARY TO CREATE A GAP BETWEEN THE REAL AND THE PERCEIVED.**

Sometimes we, too, are like that bag—needing a little bit of air here and there. There are times when it's appropriate to have a gap between who you are and who people think you are. As you already know, authenticity is the rule of the day. But *authenticity* should never mean 100 percent *transparency* in every area of your life. Transparency at the wrong time can be reckless and irresponsible. Inevitably, there will be moments when you need to project outer confidence despite inner doubts. Or, when you need to *just do it*, even when you're not sure you're entirely ready.

Airline pilots deal with this all the time. Imagine the last time you were in an airplane and you experienced turbulence. Imagine if the pilot came on the intercom and said, "Ladies and gentlemen, we're obviously experiencing some turbulence right now. I know you might be scared. I'm scared too. In fact, this is my first flight since flight school, and I'm not totally sure what to do. But please understand, I know authenticity is important, so I will continue to get on the intercom and tell you exactly what I'm thinking when I'm thinking it. Thanks, and I'm praying we have a safe flight! Oh look, the Grand Canyon is on your left!"

Short of nose-diving, that could be the worst thing a pilot could do. While that example is fictional, the scenarios below are not.[2]

An EasyJet pilot told passengers there was a 50/50 chance both its engines would work, before calling for a "show of hands" to vote whether they should stay in the terminal or take off. The pilot's announcement understandably caused instant panic, with several people demanding to be let off the plane and one becoming physically sick. EasyJet denied the events occurred. (The denial itself is an obvious issue of Authentic Leadership.)

Ryanair issued an apology after a flight attendant informed passengers over the PA system that, "We have ice on the wings, and we don't want to die." She was attempting to explain why the flight had been delayed for eight hours. The reality was that her jovial tone went over poorly. One passenger said her remarks caused "all hell to break loose" in the cabin. A Ryanair spokesperson said the "regrettable" comment was made "in the heat of the moment."

On a flight to Helsinki, a Finnish pilot said, "Ladies and gentlemen we shall be making an unscheduled landing and steep approach to Tampere airport, the plane is on fire, thank you."

And, just one more, as this is the ultimate expression of inappropriate authenticity. On a flight bound for Aberdeen, Scotland, the pilot addressed the cabin and said:

> Good afternoon gentlemen. You will have noticed that it's a bit hairy in the skies and the wind is against us. We require a steep take off out of here and it will be tricky but hold on to your seats, it's Friday night and I've got a wedding reception to go to. Over and out.

We all instinctively know that the pilot's job isn't just to fly the plane. It's to lead the passengers and crew. That means communicating confidence and calm in the service of the passengers. To communicate exactly what she's feeling when she's feeling it would ultimately be very selfish and a dereliction of her duty as a leader.

Sometimes there are moments when you need to be less than totally transparent. Sometimes it's okay for there to be a gap between what people think you feel and what you feel.

## Transparency Versus Authenticity

Learning to be an Authentic Leader includes learning the difference between transparency and authenticity. Authentic Leadership involves learning how to be the best version of yourself (not someone else) in the service of others. It means being strategically transparent, carefully considering the needs of the situation. It sometimes means being comfortable enough with what you *know* to admit what you *don't know*. That's what I saw my friend, we'll call her Katie, do.

Katie is an executive at a large hospital in Ohio. She invited me to a team meeting to speak on leadership, where I witnessed her incredibly Authentic Leadership style.

At the time Katie was new to her role and just digging into the challenges of her department. In the meeting, I watched 150 angry nurses and aides pepper her with questions about changes. Since Katie had just started there was no way she could have any satisfying answers. From where I sat, it felt like I was watching sharks circling. Everyone in the room knew she was in an uncomfortable position. It's a situation where insecurity often rears its ugly head. But Katie surprised everyone. Instead of pretending she had it together, making up an answer, or dismissing their concerns, she did the opposite. She squared her shoulders and said, "I see why you are frustrated. It makes sense. If I was in your shoes and had been through what you've been through, I would be upset too! But I don't have answers for you today. It's urgent, I know. You have my commitment that I will sit and talk with each one of you if that's what it takes to find a solution that works for you. Give me a month and you'll have answers!"

The room, once filled with anxious energy, instantly relaxed. I could literally see scowls replaced by smiles. It was impressive to see how an authentic confession of ignorance paired with a sincere commitment to results could win over a room. It took incredible confidence and skill to properly admit what she could do and what she could not do in that moment.

That's Authentic Leadership.

# CHAPTER 2

# Pretending to Be Someone Better

"Because true belonging only happens when we present our authentic, imperfect selves to the world, our sense of belonging can never be greater than our level of self-acceptance."

BRENÉ BROWN

Insecurity doesn't happen by accident. It's conceived the moment you believe you don't measure up to the people around you. It grows as you hide what you really think. It thrives when you pretend to be someone better than you really are.

Before I started high school, I had a gap. The gap wasn't caused by anything I did. It was caused by my parents. English wasn't my first language. It was Sign Language, because both my parents were deaf.

Not just one. Both.

I know, it's crazy.

## My Perceived Gap

My deaf, Nigerian immigrant parents built a life for me and my hearing siblings anyone would envy. I'm privileged to have had two incredibly accomplished and loving people as parents. The idea of two people succeeding with the cards stacked against them certainly didn't suggest *any* disability. As young adults, they arrived in the U.S. deaf and alone. After getting married in Idaho, they earned graduate degrees, built a home, and taught at the largest university in our area. Brave. Incredible. Amazing. There aren't enough words or time to explain the talent and tenacity of Tim and Sheila Owolabi.

Growing up, I wish I had felt this way.

But I didn't.

My parents raised their family in a very small town in northeast Ohio. (I'm talking you-can-hold-your-breath-and-drive-through-the-entire-town small.) Not only were we the only black family, but we were likely the only family to have two deaf parents. We were *certainly* the only black family with two deaf parents. Dalton was safe and stable in every sense, but everywhere I went—from the gas station to my homeroom—I felt like I was "the black kid with deaf parents."

And I hated it.

Mostly because I would get the same four questions.

1. How do your parents drive?
2. How do they have jobs?
3. Can they hear you swear? (That was from my friends)
4. How did you learn to talk?

I imagine we must have appeared incredibly exotic. Foreigners in every sense—in a land populated more heavily by cattle than humans. When I grew irritated from all the questions, I began to respond "I don't know. How did *you* learn to talk?" That didn't make things any better.

Whenever we were in town (meaning somewhere between the three stoplights), I was on stage. As I'd sign to my mom about preferring salami over bologna at the Block and Barrel deli counter, out of the corner of my eye I could see middle-aged men staring at us, mouths open. It drove me crazy.

When you're ten years old, stares make you think there's something horribly abnormal about you. When you're ten years old, more than anything, you want to be normal. Dalton normal. The kind of normal that included white parents *who could hear.*

I wasn't normal. I couldn't be. And, in my mind, my parents wouldn't let me.

**I INTENTIONALLY PUT A GAP
BETWEEN WHO I REALLY WAS AND
WHO PEOPLE THOUGHT I WAS.**

Instead of accepting my difference, I hid and intentionally created opportunities to put a gap between who I really was and who people thought I was. I did everything I could to cause people to see me as something different than "that black kid with the deaf parents." Then, one day I got a huge opportunity. Someone gave me a free car.

## Creating My Persona

Like most high schoolers, I spent an ungodly amount of energy projecting who I wanted people to think I was. After experiencing success on the basketball court, I spent my time investing in Dan, the high-school jock, in order to leave behind Dan, the kid with the deaf parents.

But, to complete the look, I had to get a car. When I was sixteen, it seemed like everyone had a car. If you were cool, you had a car. No question about it. So, I asked my mom and dad if they'd buy me a car. Guess what they said?

*No!* My Nigerian, deaf parents, who scratched and clawed for everything they had ever owned—with no family for support, no generational wealth, no deep social connections—said, "No." The exchange went something like this.

> ME:  When do you think I can get a car?
> MOM:  What do you need a car for?
> ME:  To drive myself to school and basketball practice.
> MOM:  Did the school bus stop working?
> ME:  No, it is running fine.

MOM: So, why do you need a car?

ME: Because, I …

MOM: How will you buy a car without a job?

ME: I thought you could buy it for …

I didn't finish my sentence before the look from my mom told me I'd better not sign another word. I put my hands in my pockets.

Tim and Sheila Owolabi knew hard work. And they weren't about to deprive me of the *joy* of scratching and clawing for my own car.

I never really listened to their reasons or explanations. All I heard, all I saw was that I wasn't getting a car.

But then one day, coach called my name after basketball practice. His name was Duane Miller. He was in his late sixties and he was the kind of guy everyone knew around town. He served everywhere he went—from school board to the elder board at the local Mennonite church. Duane had the rare ability to make you feel like you were the most talented person on earth, while also making you feel the pressure to do something extraordinary with your life. I loved him as a coach.

He had on an old tweed jacket when he called me into his office. He sat me down and looked me in the eye and said "Dan, my wife and I talked. We know you've wanted a car. We'd like to give you one for free."

I couldn't believe it! I literally jumped up and down.

I was getting a car! A. FREE. CAR. And, I didn't have to experience the supposed joy of working for it.

I immediately felt less strange and more conventional. I could fit in. A car meant I was different, but in the way that meant *special*, not *weird*. The persona was complete. I could drive my friends around and finally be independent of my family—my parents. I could leave the whole Deaf/Nigerian thing behind.

That's how I got my first car. Now, let me tell you about how I lost it.

## Was My Persona Ever Real?

It just took me a couple of weeks to start showing off and pushing the car to see what it could do. And at some point, I began bragging to my friends about how fast I could get from my bedroom to my homeroom.

Let's all just take a moment to acknowledge how desperately I must have been seeking attention and approval—affirmation and inclusion—to be seen as cool-Dan-who-gets-to-sleep-in-and-drive-to-school.

From the moment I woke up, I timed everything—taking a shower, getting dressed, eating breakfast, getting my books, driving and finally sitting in my homeroom seat. It was an exciting challenge, and it took me exactly thirteen and one-half minutes.

And every day, for some strange reason, I tried to beat my time. One day I realized that I could shave a full minute off my time if I didn't break for a stop sign near my house. It was an intersection on flat ground, except for a steep hill on the right that obscured oncoming traffic. But I knew that if I watched the crest of the hill for cars, I could get through the intersection safely without stopping. It worked. And I saved myself one more minute. Efficiency is everything for a high schooler trying to win a contest that no one is competing in.

Then one day I woke up late.

I remember feeling wildly panicked. Like an anxious tornado, I grabbed my keys, clothes, books, breakfast (I didn't even stop to shower) and jumped into my new car. I was worried about the intersection. I knew I had to hit the intersection fast to get to school on time. So, as the intersection got closer, I looked harder. I looked to my right, at the hill. Nothing. So, I didn't slow down, but I looked again, squinting.

Nothing.

I hit the gas and entered the intersection.

I was in the intersection less than a second when I saw it. Through the corner of my eye, on the *left* side, was a school bus traveling directly at me.

It hit me on the driver's side. It lifted my car three feet off the ground and into the air. I could hear the glass shattering. I could hear the metal crunching. And when my car settled, I could see the kids crying in the bus.

That's when I knew I had screwed up.

Imagine going to Duane's house. Knocking on his door. Sitting down on his couch and saying to him and his wife, "Remember that car you gave me for free? I just totaled it. Thanks for investing in me."

Or, going to your parents, who didn't want you to have the car in the first place, and saying, "Mom, Dad, I just hit a school bus and totaled my car.

I was thankful no one was seriously hurt. But it was horrible. For my sixteen-year-old mind, the worst part were the days after the accident. In such a small town, I *knew* people were talking. One day I overheard a conversation at the grocery store.

"Did you hear about the kid who hit a school bus?"

"Yea. It was that guy, you know, the black kid with two deaf parents."

And just like that, I was the black kid with deaf parents again.

My persona—the idea of who I wanted people to believe I was—the cool basketball player who transcended his hard-working, immigrant parents was wrecked. Literally.

I felt like a fraud, exposed. And it was the worst feeling of my life.

## THE TEMPTATION TO PRETEND, TO TRY TO BE SOMETHING DIFFERENT THAN WHO WE ARE, IS GREAT.

Maybe you don't have two deaf parents. Maybe the people you grew up with looked just like you. Maybe you didn't get hit by a school bus. But you understand the temptation to pretend, to try to be something different than who you are. And if you prop up a fabricated version of yourself for too long, you will be exposed.

# CHAPTER 3

# Why We Choose Inauthenticity

> "Hallo, Rabbit," he said, "is that you?"
> "Let's pretend it isn't," said Rabbit, "
> and see what happens."

A. A. MILNE

Far too often, insecure leaders create the person they think others want them to be, while never becoming the authentic person they were created to be. The masquerade is exhausting, unsustainable, and dangerous to your leadership. So why do some people choose to be inauthentic? There are a few reasons.

## Inauthenticity Protects You

Inauthenticity temporarily protects you from dealing with difficult relationships and challenging conversations. To understand how this works, there are few examples as clear as a story told by C.S. Lewis. I'm a huge fan of Lewis. His books were the first ones I read for fun. In fact, *The Great Divorce* was the very first book I read outside a high-school assignment.

In his 1945 novel, Lewis writes about people who have died, and now live in "Grey Town." Everyone in Grey Town can take a bus to "heaven." Once in heaven, the passengers meet people from their life on earth, and each encounter provides a glimpse into their character.

The title of the book comes from the idea that there's a great separation—divorce—between the Grey Town (a phrase used for hell) and the incredible joy of heaven. Every passenger on the bus is given the choice between heaven or hell. Amazingly, most choose to go back to hell! Lewis then describes the character of each person who chooses to go back to Grey Town. To understand why people embrace inauthenticity, the encounter between a woman, a Dwarf, and his Tragedian serves as a great example.

The encounter starts with the narrator observing the woman, who has been in heaven for a while. When the bus from Grey Town rolls up, she walks down to meet the passengers, ready to convince some to stay in heaven. She sees a tall man getting off the bus who she recognizes as a friend, and she's looking forward to inviting him to stay.

But as the woman walks closer and sees more clearly, she realizes three things. First, the tall man isn't her friend. In fact, her friend is a much, much smaller person (a Dwarf), quietly standing next to the tall man. Second, the tall man isn't a man at all. It is a ghost-like person resembling what her friend looked like on Earth. Third, her friend is holding a leash connected to the neck of the ghost.

The taller ghost is a loud, over-the top actor (Tragedian) who is deeply offended by something that had happened on Earth, yet he does everything he can to act like nothing is wrong. Every time he speaks, he can't help but hint about how hurt and disappointed he really is. The narrator describes their interaction as they meet outside the bus.

> She stooped down and kissed the Dwarf. It made one shudder to see her in such close contact with that cold, damp, shrunken thing. But she did not shudder. "Frank," she said, "before anything else, forgive me. For all I ever did wrong and for all I did not do right since the first day we met, I ask your pardon."
>
> The Dwarf gave her a glance, not a full look. He was watching the Tragedian out of the corner of his eyes. Then he gave a jerk to the chain: and it was the Tragedian, not he, who answered the Lady. "There, there," said the Tragedian. "We'll say no more about it. We all make mistakes." With the words there came over his features a ghastly contortion which, I think, was meant for an indulgently playful smile. "We'll say no more," he continued. "It's not myself I'm thinking about.

It is you. That is what has been continually on my mind—all these years. The thought of you—you here alone, breaking your heart about me."

"But now,' said the Lady to the Dwarf, "you can set all that aside. Never think like that again. It is all over."

Her beauty brightened so that I could hardly see anything else, and under that sweet compulsion the Dwarf really looked at her for the first time. For a second I thought he was growing more like a man. He opened his mouth. He himself was going to speak this time. But oh, the disappointment when the words came!

"You missed me?" he croaked in a small, bleating voice.

Yet even then she was not taken aback. Still the love and courtesy flowed from her.

"Dear, you will understand about that very soon," she said. "But to-day—."

What happened next gave me a shock. The Dwarf and the Tragedian spoke in unison, not to her but to one another. "You'll notice," they warned one another, "she hasn't answered our question." I realized then that they were one person, or rather that both were the remains of what had once been a person. The Dwarf again rattled the chain.

"You missed me?" said the Tragedian to the Lady, throwing a dreadful theatrical tremor into his voice.

"Dear friend," said the Lady, still attending exclusively to the Dwarf, "you may be happy about that and about everything else. Forget all about it forever."

And really, for a moment, I thought the Dwarf was going to obey: partly because the outlines of his face became a little clearer, and partly because the invitation to all joy, singing out of her whole being like a bird's song on an April evening, seemed to me such that no creature could resist it. Then he hesitated. And then-once more he and his accomplice spoke in unison.

"Of course it would be rather fine and magnanimous not to press the point," they said to one another. "But can we be sure she'd notice? We've done these sort of things before. There was the time we let her have the last stamp in the house to write to her mother and said nothing although she had known we wanted to write a letter our self. We'd thought she'd remember and see how unselfish we'd been. But she never did. And there was the time ... oh, lots and lots of times!" So the Dwarf gave a shake to the chain and—

While the woman tries repeatedly to talk directly to her friend, she can only get a response from the ghost. Eventually, she stops trying to convince her friend to be authentic and allows him to return to hell. As that encounter progresses, the Dwarf continues to diminish in size, staying in the shadow of the Tragedian. The more authority the Dwarf gives the Tragedian to speak on his behalf, the smaller the Dwarf becomes.

The image of the Dwarf using the Tragedian underscores a powerful reality. To cope with offense, disappointment, and pain, the Tragedian protected the Dwarf from addressing reality. The Tragedian's only goal was to project an image that everything was okay.

All of us have a Tragedian on a leash. And, like the Dwarf, we shrink in comparison. Instead of directly addressing uncomfortable conversations, misunderstandings, or feelings of inadequacy, we project, pretend, and act as if things are better than they are. In a word, we choose inauthenticity. When we stop striving to be authentic, we automatically default to creating personas and acting out what we want people to see. We know there's a gap between who we are and who people think we are. But closing the gap involves a lot of work and vulnerability that we would just as soon avoid.

## Discarding the Actor

Most leaders have learned how to appear strong, successful, and confident on the surface. Behind the scenes, they are anxious, defensive, and fearful of vulnerability. The first task when I work with leaders is to help them set aside the "actor" and talk to the authentic leader—warts and all.

That's a difficult process. Unless facing a personal crisis, most insecure people are very comfortable performing the role of a busy entrepreneur, working mom, heroic athlete, etc., and projecting more confidence than they really possess. This kind of inauthentic performance can color every part of your life.

> UNLESS FACING A PERSONAL
> CRISIS, MOST INSECURE PEOPLE
> ARE COMFORTABLE PERFORMING
> THE ROLE OF BUSY PERSON.

Joe DiMaggio was a prime example of how performance can consume your life. Arguably one of the greatest heroes in American baseball, DiMaggio won the adoration of millions of Americans. But privately, he battled deep insecurities. DiMaggio biographer, Jerome Charyn,[3] said, "As the New York Yankees' star centerfielder from 1936 to 1951, Joe DiMaggio is enshrined in America's memory as the epitome in sports of grace, dignity, and that ineffable quality called 'class.'"

From the outside looking in, it's easy to see why he was admired by millions; he was a record-breaking, good-looking, athletic man. DiMaggio played for the best teams, won multiple titles, and, at the dawn of WWII, held a hitting streak that had climbed to an unprecedented fifty-six consecutive games. When he finally broke the record, he was on the front page of every newspaper in the country. To top it off, he even married what culture deemed the best-looking woman of his generation, Marilyn Monroe. For the rest of his life, DiMaggio would be introduced as "the greatest living baseball player." He achieved the height of celebrity.

After his death, however, his fans learned that legendary status came at a cost. His funeral saw less than one hundred attendees. Those present—children, aunts, uncles, cousins—shared a common story: long seasons of estrangement from him, longer than his famed hitting streaks.

Years later, a scathing biography revealed the truth behind DiMaggio's life. He was far from the confident hero the public saw. Instead he was consumed by insecurities and deeply concerned himself with manufacturing and maintaining an image for the public. Ben Creamer's book, *Joe DiMaggio: The Hero's Life,*[4] explains how DiMaggio's obsession with performance and projection of "Joe the hero" led to the decay of "Joe in real life."

DiMaggio struggled in all his relationships. Aside from his road roommate, Lefty Gomez, he had no close friends. Often moody, cranky, silent, and lonely, if you dealt with DiMaggio at all, it was on his terms. Reporters knew to write him up as a hero, or he'd refuse to answer your questions or even associate with you.

Through his life, DiMaggio remained estranged from his son and his immediate family members. His first wife took their son and left him, primarily due to his neglect of the marriage. Even Marilyn Monroe quietly divorced him, once she realized he had no intention of creating a married life they could both enjoy. His intentions were to preserve an image of unity and love, not create the real thing. In fact, on their honeymoon in Japan, when young couples typically enjoy an emotional high together, Monroe cut the trip short, preferring to attend a promotional opportunity by herself. DiMaggio obliged and flew home alone, knowing that it wouldn't affect their public image.

After retirement, DiMaggio was consistently called the "Greatest Living Baseball Player." But the title was perhaps the clearest evidence of the depth of his insecurity. Rather than allow his fans and records to speak for themselves, DiMaggio created the title himself. In his thirty years of retirement, whenever he was honored, DiMaggio demanded he be introduced last—always last—and with *his* title. In one incident, at Yankee Old-Timers Day, after DiMaggio again insisted on being introduced as the "Greatest Living Baseball Player," he faced opposition. Legendary Yankee's fan, Billy Crystal, refused. DiMaggio promptly punched Crystal in the stomach. Crystal described the encounter in his book.[5]

> We were standing just outside of the Yankees clubhouse when the door opened and Joe DiMaggio came out. He stepped toward me and, without warning, punched me in the stomach. Hard. I wasn't ready for it. He put his face inches from mine. 'Greatest living player!' he hissed, and stormed off.

Insecurity often manifests itself in an ironclad grip on titles, public reputation, positions of power, inclusion in certain social circles, possessions, degrees, etc. When you have something to hide, something to prove, or something to lose you will move heaven and earth in defense of your persona. For Joe DiMaggio, his insistence on an honored title, his inability to maintain an inner circle of loved ones, or his refusal to allow reporters to have a contrary opinion of him reveal a powerful plague of insecurities. DiMaggio's quest to create a perfectly manufactured image—who he was "supposed" to be—expanded to fill every part of his life and eventually drove everything else out.

## Get Real About Insecurity

Some have learned how to keep insecurity at bay. There are people who don't succumb to the temptation to pretend and perform. Instead of crumbling under the weight of others' expectations, these people operate with a natural confidence that communicates, "Maybe I can't do everything, but here's what I can do."

The ancient writers of the Bible tell a story of a young man named Joseph, and how he dealt with the pressure to pretend. The Pharaoh, the King of Egypt, approached him to interpret a dream. The Pharaoh had just experienced a terrifying dream, but as he turned to his wisest advisors, he realized no one was able to help him understand what he saw. He said to Joseph, "I heard you can interpret dreams."

This was close to the truth. Accurately explaining the

meaning of at least two dreams before, Joseph had a track record of helping people understand what they couldn't understand on their own. He was exceptional and could have carried that mantle as an interpreter, if he wanted. But Joseph saw the trap of high expectations and surprised everyone with his answer.

He knew if the Pharaoh thought he could interpret dreams once, he would be called upon to do it other times. The reality was that Joseph had no idea how or why he was able to interpret dreams. He understood it as a pure, random gift from God. To answer "yes" would have been to feed the hype. It would have inferred that he could summon the ability at will, which he couldn't.

Turning to the Pharaoh, the most powerful person in the world, Joseph was authentically confident and straightforward. He refused to allow the Pharaoh to think of Joseph as anything more than what he was. So, he said "I cannot, but God can."

Simple as that.

I can't do that. But ask God, who I know can do it.

I can't do this, but here's what I can do.

Imagine if you said that when people hoisted expectations on you.

- I can't promise we'll go undefeated, but I can promise that I'll rally the team and we'll play our best every night.
- I can't promise this company will grow, but I can promise I'll do everything I can to help you and this company reach its fullest potential.

- I can't promise the deal will go through, but what I can promise is that we will be prepared to offer them the best we have.

## Living Up to the Hype

But take heed, the most successful people often struggle with a hidden fear that they won't live up to their own hype. Exceptional performance brings its own weight and challenges.

> EXCEPTIONAL PERFORMANCE
> BRINGS ITS OWN WEIGHT
> AND CHALLENGES.

Michael Jackson battled that pressure. I'm a fan of the music created by Jackson. Who can argue that *Thriller* was not extraordinary work? But my admiration of Jackson ends there. The more I understood his story, the more I understood the unique challenges that came because of his success. In 1982, after a moderately successful career in the music industry, Jackson released the album *Thriller*. It was an unexpected smash hit. *Thriller* set the record for the most top ten singles from a single album. Within the year, Jackson was selling a million copies per week around the world. When *Thriller* became the first album in American history to top the best seller list for two years in a row, Jackson became a musician in a class of his own. Jackson's album, music videos, and concerts crowned him the "King of Pop" and, subsequently, his exploding global fanbase clamored for more music of the same caliber as *Thriller*. But, after decades of striving and a few solid albums, Jackson died. He was unable to reproduce anything close to the smashing success of *Thriller*.

Years later, Jackson's friend, Oprah Winfrey, reflected on how he handled the expectation to produce. She said:[6]

> I started reading this incredible article about Michael Jackson [in *Vanity Fair*], and one of Jackson's friends was quoted as saying, "His number-one problem is that he never realized that *Thriller* was a phenomenon. And he spent the rest of his life trying to chase it." And so, when *Bad* only sold—*only sold*—20 million albums early on, he was disappointed because it wasn't *Thriller*. He thought he was going to top *Thriller*. I went, Whoa. Pay attention to that. I didn't want to be the person chasing a phenomenon.

Sometimes the most successful people battle the challenge of living up to their own hype. Sometimes our insecurities come from the expectation to reproduce something that isn't reproducible. When we experience success, the gap between who you are and who people think you are can grow quickly and unexpectedly. That can create a tremendous degree of inner insecurity. Moreover, the most dangerous leaders are insecure leaders. Instead of using their position to serve their customers, their organization, or their team, these leaders will use their platform to protect their manufactured image at all costs.

# PART TWO

# The Authentic Leader

# CHAPTER 4

# Authentic Confidence

"Those that don't got it, can't show it.
Those that got it, can't hide it."

ZORA NEALE HURSTON

The ability to be authentic doesn't happen in an instant. It takes confidence, developed over time, to be yourself and avoid the impulse to project or pretend. Authentic confidence is an indispensable quality of an Authentic Leader, and it comes from seasons of testing and challenge that produce a deep sense of self-worth. Recently I learned an example of how to develop authentic confidence, from the story of how my mom came to America.

## Building Self-Confidence

I don't remember when I realized having two deaf, immigrant parents was unique. But, at some point I realized other kids didn't interpret for their parents at Walmart or had grandparents who lived on another continent. But I *do* remember the day I asked my mom how she came to the United States, how she became a college professor, and how she became the chair of her department. Practically speaking, I knew my mom and dad overcame *many challenges* to create a life in America, but I never knew exactly what she faced. Once I heard her whole story, I became more convinced in the power of authenticity. I understood how developing authentic confidence can give you the energy to lead through the most daunting challenges in life.

While other leaders tend to hide their flaws, there was no way for Sheila Owolabi to hide her deafness. My mother became a leader, and a tremendous one at that, by being her authentic self. As I write this, she's in the middle of teaching a heavy course load as a professor at the University of Louisville. In her twenty-five-year teaching career, she's led thousands of students and dozens of faculty. She's launched new programs and mentored new instructors. And she did all of this as a middle-aged black woman who can't hear.

If you observed her teach American Sign Language, you'd see that she is a master at non-verbal communication. She uses her entire body to act out hilarious stories, and uses the whiteboard to help teach challenging content. She has extraordinary lip-reading skills, carries a pad of paper to communicate with new students one on one, and she understands how to make you feel like the most important person in the room. If you were wondering, "How does a deaf person teach a college class?" That's how she does it.

But if you're wondering the bigger, more important question, "How does someone with such obvious disadvantages gain the confidence to lead at that level?" I wondered that too. When I asked, she told me she found her confidence before she left Nigeria.

### *First, Start with Low Expectations*

My mother, Sheila Owolabi, was born in Nigeria in 1954, second youngest in a family of nine children. By her sixth birthday, she was permanently deaf, a result of complications from contracting smallpox.

Now, let's pause here. Imagine you're in Nigeria in the early 1960s. Your family is poor. You are just one of nine other siblings. You're a girl. Oh, and you're deaf too. What are your chances of living a life full of confidence?

If you had asked my mom, she would have told you what you already know. Her life was a struggle. Kids in the neighborhood made fun of her. Her own parents didn't even bother to learn sign language. She was, essentially, written off.

She failed her freshmen year of high school and needed to repeat the grade. She then failed her sophomore year and needed to repeat that grade. Then, she failed her junior year, and, you guessed it, she repeated that grade too. Finally, because she was so much older than her fellow students, her teachers convinced her to take a certificate of completion and leave high school before she started her senior year.

Her friends and family assumed she'd live with her parents the rest of her life. Expectations were low. No one expected her to marry or do anything besides, maybe, a service job. My mom started to believe that as well. Then one day, everything changed.

She attended a newly formed youth group for deaf students in Lagos, Nigeria. There, she met Andrew Foster, an American and Christian missionary who traveled through Africa, launching schools dedicated to empowering deaf students, a neglected and underserved population. Foster dedicated extraordinary energy to identifying and investing in the most promising deaf young adults. He was a tall, smart African-American teacher, who was also deaf.

With a graduate degree from the United States, Foster was easily the most accomplished deaf person anyone in Lagos had ever seen. But the first day my mother met Foster, he saw something in her. He said, "Do you realize how intelligent you are? You're sharper than most hearing kids!"

By that time she was twenty-two, and it was the *first time* anyone told her she was smart. As you can imagine, she beamed.

After working with her for months, Foster told my mother about a scholarship that the Nigerian Government offered to young people with disabilities. The grant provided disabled Nigeran students free tuition to American universities and colleges. Foster encouraged her to apply. That's all the motivation she needed.

### Second, Add Motivation

She went to the government office. It was just like it was in those eighties-era movies about overseas government offices. The waiting room was hot, crowded, and dusty. A rickety fan swung from the ceiling. She sat down on a squeaky, three-foot wooden bench in the corner and waited.

When it was her turn, she was ushered into an office. An overweight government official began talking, presumably about the scholarship and the application process. But my mom stopped him. She pointed to her ears and said as clearly as she could manage, "I can't hear."

The moment he understood she was deaf, his countenance changed. He shifted in his seat, gave a nervous smile, and motioned for her to leave his office and wait in the lobby. She complied, assuming he just needed to sort some things out and would call her back in shortly. He didn't.

She waited until she was the last person in the lobby, watching that same man put on his coat and lock his office behind him. When he turned around, he was surprised to see her still there.

"Come back tomorrow," he said loudly, over-enunciating.

So, the next day, she came back. Only to sit in the lobby, again. She didn't get an interview. She waited until she was the last person in the lobby. Again, the man came out and told her to come back the next day.

Only for the same thing to happen for the third day in a row.

She realized she was being had. It was much easier to communicate with a person in a wheelchair than to work with a deaf woman. The man didn't want to help her.

But she refused to give up. In fact, she came back to that office every week for two years.

*Two years!*

### Third, Mix in Determination

By any measure, that's an extraordinary display of patience and perseverance. But it was her only option. While she had been brushed aside and overlooked every week, she had not yet been denied the scholarship. In those two years, my mom learned a new definition of determination. This opportunity was too big to allow her insecurities to get in the way. She would simply *show up* for as long as it took for someone to give her a straight answer.

Then, one day, she came into the office and looked at the counter. The man—that man—wasn't there. Instead, a woman greeted her. The woman across the counter grabbed a sheet of paper and wrote, "Are you the deaf woman who's been coming here for *two years*? I'm so sorry! The man who was here before retired last week. I'm the new director, and I want to help you!"

### Finally, Confidence is Born!

After two years, it all happened for her—in one day. Within twenty-four hours she got a visa, a passport, and a ticket to the United States. She'd be leaving the following week.

She ran home to tell her family, but no one believed her. She had been talking about this alleged opportunity for twenty-four months and had nothing to show for it. And now, all of a sudden, she was leaving?!

She didn't care if they didn't believe her. She packed her dresses, shoes, and whatever else she could fit in a few suitcases. When the day came for her to leave, a small crowd of family and friends gathered at her house. Some still didn't believe she was about to go to America. How would she work? Who did she know? Where would she live?

My mom didn't answer their questions. She was confident she could figure it out. So, she said her goodbyes, promised to write, and hopped on a plane to America.

Looking back, few made her path easy. Nobody stepped in to help her communicate. For two years! Not her parents, her friends, or the government. Alone most of the time, she wondered if she was just wasting her time. If this was simply what her life was supposed to be.

But she decided to focus on what her life *could* be instead.

## OVERCOMING CHALLENGES UNLOCKS CONFIDENCE TO OVERCOME EVEN GREATER CHALLENGES.

Overcoming those challenges unlocked her confidence to overcome even greater challenges. Enduring repeated rejection for two years taught her the rewards of perseverance. Her capacity to fight increased. She learned that if she trusted God and stayed with something long enough, big things could happen.

Looking back, my mother considered those two years of waiting the most formative years of her life as they provided so many important lessons in authentic confidence. She would employ that newfound confidence when she worked for her bachelor's degree, her master's degree, and when she started teaching at the university level. From that dusty, hot, administrative government office in Lagos to the first classroom where she taught at Kent State University, she never pretended to be anyone but herself. She owned her experience and stood confidently in it.

## Natural Confidence

The ability to be authentic is born from naturally acquired confidence. It comes from the belief that you have enough, and you *are* good enough.

- Good enough to meet the challenge in front of you.
- Good enough to figure it out.
- Good enough to connect with others.
- Good enough to reveal your real thoughts and your true self to others.

That kind of natural confidence only develops after you've wrestled self-doubt to the ground. It comes after you've endured challenges without quitting or compromising. It comes after you've evaluated your weaknesses with clear eyes and learned how to succeed in spite of them.

But it's more than that. People with authentic confidence have a different foundation. They know their identity, and it is not tethered to what others think. While they might enjoy the praise of others and look forward to achieving their goals, their self-worth isn't determined by any of those things.

Their life, their work is based on something much greater.

As someone who has found tremendous strength from my faith, I've recognized the value of placing my identity in something deeper than external accomplishments or the applause of a crowd. As a Christian I fundamentally believe that, whether I succeed or fail, God still loves me, and I find my ultimate identity in my relationship with Christ. And that gives me the foundation, the authentic confidence to attempt anything.

### Tale of Two Builders

One of my favorite things about Jesus is that he told a lot of stories. Sometimes it seems like that's all he did. One of his best-known stories is about two homebuilders, and it's also about creating authentic confidence. Like most of Jesus' stories, there are a few interpretations. This version is my favorite.

The first builder begins the process of building the house by carefully looking for a strong foundation. He looks and finds solid rock, but it's buried deep underneath a thick layer of sand. It's going to take much more time and extra work to dig through the sand to get to the rock. Even then, he'll still need to dig into the rock to begin construction. But this builder has some foresight. He decides the effort is worth it and starts digging.

The second builder also begins by identifying the best spot for the home. He finds a spot, close to the first builder, that also has a thick layer of sandy topsoil. But he's not convinced that he needs to dig a foundation as deep as his neighbor. He digs a foundation into the sand, but stops when he hits the rock.

Both homes are finished and, being in the same neighborhood, they both look incredible at street level. Both builders feel confident that they've done their best, and feel proud of what they've built.

Years later, a massive storm hits the neighborhood. In the torrential downpour, rivers rise, the wind howls, and both homes take a beating. When the storm passes, one home is conspicuously untouched. The first builder emerges from his house and looks around at his neighborhood. Immediately he's thankful that he made the extra effort to build the four corners of his house deep into the rock below. His house stood strong in the storm. But his neighbor's home, with a shallow foundation, completely collapsed.

That's the nature of authentic confidence. It's knowing that your foundation runs deeper than people understand. It's knowing your most difficult seasons, your divorce, your diagnosis, your bankruptcy or your years of unemployment have given you the gift of resilience. It's knowing you certainly didn't enjoy the season of challenge, but you're now enjoying the confidence that comes after it. It's the feeling that, though storms may come and the rain may fall, you will not be knocked down. Authentic confidence is living in a neighborhood full of houses built on sand, knowing yours is built on bedrock.

# CHAPTER 5

# Nothing to Hide, Nothing to Prove, and Nothing to Lose

"Do not judge me by my successes,
judge me by how many times I fell
down and got back up again."

NELSON MANDELA

Becoming an Authentic Leader isn't about learning new information, it's about unlearning old habits. It's about peeling back the layers of doubt that prevent you from becoming the leader God intended you to be. At the core, Authentic Leadership is a journey back to the best version of yourself. Before fear, pride, or insecurity became stumbling stones. With that in mind, it's helpful to remind yourself of three truths about yourself: You have nothing to hide, nothing to prove, and nothing to lose.

## Remind Yourself You Have Nothing to Hide

Leading others when you don't have the experience you need or the knowledge you'd like can be terrifying. That's why when leaders hide, they tend to conceal their lack of experience first. But, it's helpful to remember that gaining the necessary knowledge and experience is a process. One of my favorite TV scenes is from *The West Wing*, and it illustrates the process of gaining experience. Explaining her time working in the White House, a woman said,[7]

> There are three phases you go through when working for the White House.
>
> First, you're brand new. You feel lucky to be there. You see big people, famous people. You tell yourself, "You got in by a fluke. Keep your head down. Don't say anything stupid. Do your best."
>
> Second, you've been there for about a year. You've done some work. You understand how things work. You have some friends. You realize this is a huge blessing, but you think, "I feel equal to these people."
>
> Finally, you understand nearly everything. You see how frail we are. You know how half dumb or fully dumb we are. And you say to yourself, "Holy Cow! We're the ones running the country?!

Becoming an Authentic Leader is a process, and it starts by realizing it's okay to feel stupid at first. Everyone feels that way when they start. You must remind yourself not to hide the fact that you don't know everything. It's true, when you step out into an unknown environment, mistakes will happen. It's true, when you're surrounded by more experienced people, you will give the wrong answer. You will feel embarrassed. Count on it.

## AUTHENTIC LEADERS ARE CONSTANT LEARNERS, AND THEY DON'T HIDE THAT FACT.

But it's *also* true that with time, focus, and intentionality, you will grow. So never hide that you don't know something or act like you have more experience than you do. I'm not suggesting you walk around declaring *everything* you don't know. Use discretion. Instead, I'm saying Authentic Leaders are constant learners, and they don't hide that fact. They ask questions and have an obvious posture of curiosity. They don't try to be know-it-alls, rather they strive to be a learn-it-all. And even though you'll battle insecurity when you don't know as much as you'd like, and feel like everyone knows more than you, remind yourself not to hide. Then one day you'll learn enough to actually solve a problem, and you'll gain a new level of confidence. You'll say, "Maybe I don't know it, but I can learn it!"

Steve Jobs once said,[8]

> Life can be so much broader, once you dis-
> cover one simple fact: Everything around you
> that you call "life" was made up by people
> that were no smarter than you—and you can
> change it. You can influence it …

Once you realize that truth, the world becomes bigger.
You start to give yourself more time to learn and more space
to make mistakes. And you see many more problems, but you
also see those problems as solvable. In fact, you might even
see yourself as the person to solve them.

## Remind Yourself You Have Nothing to Prove

Most people have an image of what a leader looks like. In fact,
when they think of a leader most people imagine someone
different than themselves. They feel like leadership is living
up to that imaginary "someone"—someone older, someone
taller, someone smarter, someone with more experience.
That someone with the pair of pants that never appear wrinkled or too short or too long. The just-right pants people.
Well, it's not just about pants. And it's not about comparing
yourself to an imaginary leader. It's about leading.

There's a big difference between the desire to lead and
the desire to be viewed as a leader. Authentic Leaders don't
sit down and one day decide that they're going to be a leader.
They aren't trying to *prove* their leadership abilities to anyone.
They just start encouraging others to think and act differently.

People, in their own time, come to consider them a leader. It's always about the goal and never about the role. Authentic Leaders make at least three decisions as they begin to lead others.

First, an Authentic Leader sees a problem and decides to take ownership of it. You're awakened with an urgency to take action—a problem, an injustice, a challenge, or an opportunity that is big enough to warrant your immediate and substantial investment of time, talent, and treasure. Seeing an urgent problem is always the beginning of leadership.

The most effective leaders in history were shaped by an urgent problem.

- Something for which they held personal convictions.
- Something that was bigger than they were.
- Something that required them to exert so much effort that they were driven to develop new courage and sharper skills in order to tackle the problem.

Winston Churchill was motivated to win WWII. Abraham Lincoln was motivated to win the Civil War. Nelson Mandela was motivated to end Apartheid. Repeatedly, history has demonstrated that the greatest challenges create the greatest leaders. Those who identify a pressing problem and are motivated to take action are the ones who authentically earn the right to be the leader.

Next, Authentic Leaders decide to rally others to help solve the problem. You can feel the burden to address an urgent challenge, but without inviting others to help you, you're simply a lone crusader. The moment you understand you can't tackle the problem on your own and you need the contribution of others is the instant you begin to become a leader.

> REPEATEDLY, HISTORY HAS
> DEMONSTRATED THAT THE
> GREATEST CHALLENGES CREATE
> THE GREATEST LEADERS.

Finally, Authentic Leaders decide to learn how to maximize the talent and energy of the group to help them solve the problem and get results together. This involves a ton of hard work. You can have an inspiring problem to solve, and inspire a tribe of people to help you solve it, but unless you learn to manage others, create reliable systems, and learn to be predictable and inspirational, you won't get far. Ronald Regan agreed. In an interview with Mike Wallace of *60 Minutes*, he said, "The greatest leader is not necessarily the one who does the greatest things. He is the one that gets the people to do the greatest things."[9] These are all things an Authentic Leader learns.

## Remind Yourself You Have Nothing to Lose

Leading with nothing to lose is leading from a mindset of surrender. It means you have given up the dream of an easy, comfortable life and have come to terms with the pain and loss that might be associated with leadership. Friends might turn on you. You might lose money. You might make embarrassing mistakes. People might talk about you. (People will *definitely* talk about you!) If you have nothing to lose, you've already added up the price of leadership and you've chosen to pay the cost because the benefit far outweighs any challenge you might face. When you lead from a mindset of surrender, you have nothing to lose.

I understood the value of surrender when I went polar bear swimming for the first time. When I was nine, my parents sent me to Boys Camp, a week long summer camp for hundreds of elementary boys. I had never been away from home for so long, and I had no clue what to expect. Between the new friends, new freedom, and new setting, Boys Camp turned out to be an absolute thrill! The best part of the week came during polar bear swimming. On the last day of camp, we woke up at six o'clock in the morning and headed to the pond. It was huge and freezing! That's the polar bear part. We got up in the dark to dare ourselves to swim in freezing cold water. No need to call child services. We enjoyed it.

As you can imagine, we had gotten to know each other through the week. By now we were comrades, taunting each other in order to get someone else to jump in first. In a bunch, we slowly walked into the pond. Toes. Then ankles. Then knees, then waist. We all wanted to swim, but no one was quite ready to totally surrender to the water. It took forever, and it was excruciating.

Then, suddenly one boy surrendered to the water. He started running, high stepping toward the deep water, and dove in while the rest of us stared.

As we watched him decide and act, I instantly knew he was smarter and braver than me. While his body was underwater adjusting to the temperature, those of us above water were still freezing and hoping the pain would slowly go away.

Seconds later, we all jumped in after him.

> SURRENDER TO SOME MOMENTARY
> PAIN, THEN YOU CAN LEAD WITH
> FAR MORE COURAGE.

Too many leaders lead like that. Filled with anxiety and insecurity, they fearfully inch toward decisions that should be made decisively. They wring their hands over the consequences of one choice versus another. They fret over what others might think, or the risk they might take on. Leading with nothing to lose means surrendering any pretense that you can become an effective leader without making hard decisions. Like polar bear swimming, if you've already surrendered to the idea that some momentary pain will be involved, then you can lead with far more courage.

## Evolving into an Authentic Leader

Reminding yourself that you have nothing to hide, nothing to prove, and nothing to lose is the beginning. After understanding how to lead with less insecurity, you must also become the kind of person that can earn trust, inspire, and

effectively lead. Part Three of this book will help you understand the process of becoming an Authentic Leader. There
are four stages (see Figure 1).

1.  **Understanding Yourself** (smallest circle): Under-
    standing who you are inside, and how you're perceived
    outside.
2.  **Leading Yourself** (slightly larger circle): Devel-
    oping the self-discipline to consistently deliver
    results, regardless of unfavorable or unpredictable
    circumstances.
3.  **Understanding Others** (even larger circle): Creat-
    ing genuine, effective influence with others by
    understanding their needs and serving them.
4.  **Leading Others** (largest circle): Creating an inspiring,
    positive vision of a preferred future and boldly calling
    people to join you in creating it.

While the first step is the smallest, it is at the core of the
whole process. Every succeeding stage grows larger and
builds on it.

**Figure 1** **The Four Stages in Becoming an Authentic Leader**

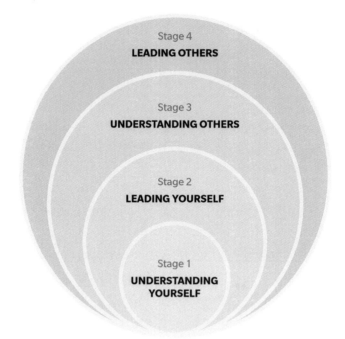

Stage 4
**LEADING OTHERS**

Stage 3
**UNDERSTANDING OTHERS**

Stage 2
**LEADING YOURSELF**

Stage 1
**UNDERSTANDING YOURSELF**

# PART THREE

# Becoming an
# Authentic Leader

# CHAPTER 6

# Understanding Yourself

## *Tell the Right Story*

> "The most important aspect of leading is knowing oneself. Know yourself, know the people around you, and then get on with it."
>
> MERVYN DAVIES, BRITISH
> MINISTER OF STATE

Possessing a solid understanding of yourself, or self-knowledge, is the foundation of Authentic Leadership. It is the first stage in the process and while it may pose a challenge for many people, looking inwardly involves only yourself.

Authentic literally means to author your own story. Self-knowledge is obtained when you take time to understand who you are, weaving together the disparate parts of your history, and create a narrative that you can own. It's understanding yourself so well that the doubts, categorizations, and opinions of others simply do not stick. As the author of your own story, you know where you've been, who you are, and where you're going in life. But, if you don't author your own story, there are plenty of people lining up to write it for you.

## The Stories We Tell Ourselves

Leaders are, by default, storytellers. They tell stories of potential and possibility. They tell stories to motivate people to create the future. They help people interpret the past and move forward. But the most important story that leaders tell is the one they tell themselves.

AUTHENTIC LEADERS UNDERSTAND
THE *CHALLENGES* IN THEIR PAST; THIS
SHAPES THEIR FUTURE *COURAGE*.

Whether you realize it or not, you have a story you tell yourself about yourself. It's a story about how far you can go in life, or what happiness means, or how past events will affect your future results. These stories are powerful and can affect whether you are or remain authentic—which means it is incredibly important to critique these stories for accuracy. Authentic Leaders have the pen in their hand

and actively write their own story. By telling the right story about their strengths and weaknesses, they develop the confidence to authentically lead. More specifically, the way they understand the *challenges* in their past has the power to shape their future *courage.*

## Story of an Underdog

The story of David and Goliath is *the* classic underdog story, and an example of the authentic confidence that comes from telling yourself the right story about your strengths.[10]

David was an unknown teenager in Israel when he traveled from his hometown to visit his older brothers on the frontlines of a battle between the Israelites and the Philistines. The Israelite army was camped across a valley from the Philistine army but had not advanced for days. The Philistines sent their towering giant, Goliath, forward to issue an extraordinary challenge. Israel was to choose their best warrior to fight Goliath; if the Israelite warrior killed Goliath, the Philistines would surrender; if Goliath killed the warrior, the Israelites would surrender. Day after day Goliath taunted Israel from across the valley. With the fate of the entire nation on the line, Israel didn't have a warrior with the courage to accept the challenge.

On the day David arrived in the camp, Goliath had shouted another challenge. But where David's brothers and the rest of the Israelite army lacked the courage to confront the giant, David was instantly infuriated. In a moment, he resolved to fight Goliath.

Grabbing a few stones and his sling, David approached the giant with incredible confidence. On his first shot, David hit Goliath in the forehead, effectively killing him.

That's a familiar story to many. The relevant question you need to ask is this, "What would give a teenager, with zero military experience, more courage than the most seasoned warriors in Israel? Where did he get the confidence to step on the battlefield and face Goliath?"

To answer that question, it's important to look at David's life before he faced off against Goliath. A closer look shows that his extraordinary courage didn't suddenly spring up in the moment he heard Goliath's challenge. Rather, his courage came from how he authored his own story.

### David Wrote his Story

Before David met Goliath, he was shaped by a crucible. This can be understood as a situation where an individual endures a severe, often painful, trial that leads to either the creation of a newfound sense of self or a significant diminishment of self-confidence. Crucibles are always a turning point in life, and never leave you the same. As David was attempting to gain permission to fight Goliath, here's how he explained his crucible to Saul, the king of Israel.

> David said to Saul, "Your servant was tending his father's sheep. When a lion or a bear came and took a lamb from the flock, I went out after him and attacked him, and rescued it from his mouth; and when he rose up against me, I seized him by his beard and struck him and killed him.

> Your servant has killed both the lion and
> the bear; and this uncircumcised Philistine
> will be like one of them, since he has taunted
> the armies of the living God.

Essentially David is saying, "I don't need to pretend that I'm tougher than I am. I don't need to try to be someone else. I've been challenged before, and I'm better and stronger because of it. I know who I am. I know my strengths, and I know I'm good enough. I beat the lion, and I beat the bear. And I'll beat this too."

Crucibles have a way of giving us a courage that others don't understand. David didn't ask for a test. He didn't invite the lion or the bear into his life. He wasn't expecting the fight, and certainly didn't enjoy the experience. But he faced the ordeal head on, and that posture of offense led him to eventually triumph. When the moment came to fight Goliath, David simply remembered his own story. His past predicament supplied remarkable confidence and helped him see himself as someone who could beat the odds. He likely told himself, "People like me can do things like this." He told himself the right story about himself.

This is a critical point. David did not simply defeat the lion and the bear. He interpreted and internalized past events in a way that positioned him for future victory.

## Authoring Your Own Story

In your life, you will face trials. Most often, you first must conquer your inner voices before you can fight the external battle. The story you tell yourself *about* your trial can carry more significance and effect than the trial itself. Learning the wrong lesson from a struggle can keep you stuck and prevent you from using it to develop authentic courage.

David's fight with the lion and the bear could have made him insecure about fighting again. He experienced a real fight with a wild animal and no doubt got roughed up. He might have even broken a bone or two. He could have been scarred for the rest of his life. We don't know how much David suffered in order to defeat the lion and the bear. So, we can understand how he might have otherwise seen the victory as something that happened by accident. That he barely escaped with his life. He could have kicked himself for carelessly letting his sheep roam close to wild animals—not just once, but twice!

David decided not to dwell on the difficulties. Instead, he authored his own story and chose to focus on the victory. He was someone who legitimately killed a lion *and* a bear. No one could take that confidence from him.

The reality is, only you know how difficult your crucibles were. Only you appreciate what it took to show up at the next family reunion after your divorce. Only you understand how hard it was to put your life back together after bankruptcy. Only you know what it feels like to launch a new business after your last one failed. Only you grasp how hard it is to get out of bed each day during chemotherapy treatments. David survived two traumatic encounters with wild animals. And that crucible emboldened him to face the future and, as we know, do the impossible.

You might have had your own figurative fights in life. Sometimes adversity can be so traumatic that you're left with your own type of PTSD in the aftermath. You become overly cautious and fearful because you're afraid you'll enter a similar period again.

Here's the point. You've experienced hurdles, just like David. David decided to see the battles with the lion and bear as positive experiences. He chose to write his own story as a victor, not the victim. There were other stories he could have written about that moment in his life, but he chose the story that provided him confidence for the future.

**LEAN INTO EACH CRUCIBLE. SEIZE THE OPPORTUNITY. WITHSTAND CHALLENGES AND KEEP MOVING.**

What has defined you? Do you remember when your parents split up? When you got the diagnosis? When your first employee quit? When you were fired? Every moment shapes how we see ourselves. Authentic Leaders lean into each crucible and seize the opportunity to see themselves as someone who can withstand challenges and keep moving. When you see your crucible as a positive, growing experience, instead of a negative, limiting experience, you're on your way to becoming an Authentic Leader.

## They Already Know Your Flaws

Self-understanding enables you to recognize your strengths, but it also goes beyond that and helps you embrace your weaknesses. Every leader has a serious weakness. I mean, stuff so serious that if exposed in the wrong situation or left unchecked could destroy the credibility of the leader and their work. The first step is to recognize your weakness. Now, some of you may say, "Dan, I don't have a weakness like *that*." But what is important to remember is that serious weaknesses never begin as serious. It is a minor issue that went unchecked. So, again, recognize your weakness.

But that's not enough. Authentic Leaders must embrace their weakness(es) as an unfortunate, but unavoidable pitfall of being human. In other words, recognizing you're not perfect. That's okay. At the end of the day, everyone—whether you realize it or not—already knows about your weakness. And, if they don't now, they will.

*New York Times* bestselling author, John Maxwell,[11] tells about a conversation he had with a CEO after a keynote speech. Maxwell spoke about identifying and exposing personal weaknesses. The CEO came up to him privately and said, "I can't tell my team my weaknesses. It'll ruin my credibility!"

John looked at him and quickly said "That's not your real problem. Your real problem is that you think they don't already know your weaknesses!"

Authentic Leaders are under no delusions about "successfully" hiding weaknesses. They embrace them, expose them, and, in the process, remove potential for catastrophe. "But, how do you do this?" you ask. How do you remove the destructive power from your weaknesses? The following example is the best I've seen.

In 2002, audiences across the country were exposed to an unlikely story of triumph in the movie *8 Mile*.[12] The award-winning film follows white rapper B-Rabbit (played by real-life rapper, Eminem) and his attempt to launch a rap career in a genre dominated by African Americans. Eminem won an Oscar for the title song, "Lose Yourself" while his character B-Rabbit won the hearts of millions with one incredible scene.

B-Rabbit is from the roughest part of Detroit. As an outsider in the African American rap community, he experiences a slew of unfortunate events during the movie. Faced with opportunities to give up on his dream, he refuses and shows up for a famous rap battle at a local club. As head-to-head competitions, rap battles are designed to humiliate opponents with lyrical insults. The crowd serves as judge, listening for the most insulting contestant and determining the winner. When he competes in the battle, B-Rabbit faces opposition from every side. Not only from his on-stage opponents, but also the crowd, who constantly remind him of his alleged weaknesses—he's too skinny, too poor, too dumb, too white to win.

In front of a packed room, B-Rabbit successfully advances in the tournament, outperforming the city's best rappers while ignoring constant racist insults and jeers. When he enters the championship round, he does something nobody expects. He turns the tables and embraces his perceived weaknesses while exposing the hidden weaknesses of his opponent. Here's what he says:

> I know everything he's got to say against
>     me. I am white. I am a bum. I do live in a
>     trailer with my mum. I did get jumped,
>     by all six of you chumps...
> but I know something about you.
> You went to Cranbrook. That's a private
>     school!
> What's the matter, dog? You embarrassed?
> This guy's not a gangster... his real name
>     is Clarence.
> Clarence lives at home with both parents,
>     and his parents have a real good marriage.

The crowd goes wild. His opponent is speechless. B-Rabbit wins the tournament. In the process, B-Rabbit teaches an incredible truth in dramatic fashion: when you understand, embrace, and expose your weaknesses, especially at the right time, in the right way, your weaknesses lose the power to be a weapon against you. Where others considered his race and income level weaknesses, B-Rabbit chose not to believe that story. Instead he owned the reality of his situation, authored his own authentic story, and determined his future. Identifying and owning your weakness effectively weakens its power to derail your growth as a leader.

UNDERSTAND, EMBRACE, AND
EXPOSE YOUR WEAKNESSES—AT THE
RIGHT TIME, IN THE RIGHT WAY—YOUR
WEAKNESSES LOSE THE POWER TO
BE A WEAPON AGAINST YOU.

## Self-Awareness

There are two types of self-awareness: internal self-awareness and external self-awareness. Internal self-awareness is understanding yourself at a deep level, while external self-awareness is understanding how others view you. Neither type develops naturally, but both are critical for your success as a leader. Let's look at them separately.

### *External Self-Awareness*

External self-awareness is a lot like trying to read the label of a bottle from the inside. You're so close to yourself, you can't fully perceive yourself.

However difficult it can be, those who understand how others see them develop behaviors that help others feel more comfortable around them. These leaders have stronger relationships as they can quickly identify the actions that jeopardize interpersonal trust. They avoid tone-deaf comments or unintentionally irritating others by making quick adjustments.

Self-awareness is critical to understanding yourself. But

it's frustratingly easy to have the wrong impression of how people feel about you.

For years, I never fully understood what others felt when they were around me. I'm a six-foot-four-inch, two-hundred-and-fifty-pound African American man. I've been tall my whole life—I've also been black my whole life. That's all I've ever known. I understand for some, being a tall, African American isn't a source of confidence. I know there can be a lot of baggage that comes with being a black male in America. However, I have had a different experience. It feels perfectly normal for me to walk most places and feel a sense of confidence. I'm rarely physically intimidated by anyone.

Recently, I was in a conversation with a travel expert about an upcoming trip to Nicaragua. I'd been told that it would be smart to get a bodyguard while I was there, due to the social and political unrest. But, when I explained the advice I'd heard, the travel expert looked me up and down and said, "You don't need a Nicaraguan bodyguard. If you did, you'd probably end up protecting him!" As I travel around the world with Branches Worldwide,[13] I've quickly realized there isn't a place on the planet that I can go to avoid turning heads.

But it wasn't until my late twenties that I realized how intimidating it can feel for people to stand next to me. I was in a meeting with a former NFL player. We were speaking at the same event. He was sitting across the table from me. He was six-foot-five and easily weighed fifty pounds more than me. When the meeting ended and we both stood up to leave, I felt something strange. It was a sense of anxiety with a hint of defensiveness. After I left the building, I reflected on the feeling. I realized that feeling was the feeling of physical intimidation!

I walked away from the meeting thinking, "Is that how my wife and friends felt when they first met me?" I went home and asked Erica. To my surprise, she said yes! She also felt that way about other men on a regular basis.

I wish the world was a place where everybody saw you for who you are on the inside. Whether you're six-foot-four and black or five-foot-two and white, I wish people understood your appearance as a mere part of the whole. We don't live in that world. It's likely we'll never live in that world. People will make judgments based on what you wear, what you look like, and how you carry yourself.

Authentic Leaders don't guess how others see them. They cultivate honest relationships with people who are willing to tell them the truth—and they ask them for it regularly. I knew one leader who scheduled quarterly one-on-one meetings with four different trusted friends. She used those meetings to ask for candid feedback about everything from the way she treated her spouse to the way she dressed, to her social media posts. Regardless of the method you use to understand how others perceive you, you would be well served to develop behaviors that put others at ease and build trust immediately.

### Internal Self-Awareness

Internal self-awareness is clearly identifying and naming your values and aspirations as well as understanding the external forces that shape your internal compass.

Internal self-awareness helps leaders take control of their thoughts and actions. Early in my leadership, I understood how important internal self-awareness was, so I began to journal. I had a spotty track record at first, but I gained momentum after a few weeks. A few years after journaling, I decided to look back over my journals to see what patterns emerged. I was shocked at what I read. I was shocked how clear the pattern was.

It turned out that every two months or so, I would write a long rambling essay about how busy I was. In each instance, I repeatedly claimed there was too much on my plate and that I didn't think I'd be able to get it all done. I wrote about how scared I was that I would miss deadlines. And, in each of those, and there were about eight or nine total entries, I would swear that I would get more control over my calendar. I would tell people "no" more often. I would become more organized. I would never let this happen again!

But then, you guessed it, I forgot. Just eight weeks later I was right back at the same place, writing about how I never wanted to be this busy again. What is the definition of insanity again? Oh, right, doing the same dang thing over and over, expecting a different result. Heaven help me.

After I read that, I had an epiphany. I understood that I could be driven by unconscious patterns of thought. It was humbling to realize I was more predictable than I thought. Since then, I learned to schedule time blocks, say "no" more often, and create monthly, weekly, and daily priority lists. Each of those steps helped me control my tendency to spontaneously over commit and thus avoid the overwhelming feeling of busyness. But without that written record exposing my unconscious habits, I likely would have continued journaling every two months about how unbelievably busy my life was.

To become more self-aware, codify your thoughts. Write them down. I know of one leader who records a vlog of herself three or four times a week, explaining how she's feeling and what she's doing. That way she's able to look back and see exactly what she looks like and what her facial expressions were on any given day because there are certain things that even black ink on white paper won't tell you. When you see your face months after, it's easier to see the strain or stress or sadness. This doesn't need to be for anyone but yourself. No need to post on LinkedIn. There's a time for that. This is not that time. This is for personal introspection. Not for leads. If you struggle to identify patterns, consider finding a friend, accountability group, or a therapist who can identify those patterns for you.

## Your Future Self

Internal and external self-awareness are significant tools that can help you lead from a place of authenticity. Another significant step towards knowing yourself is knowing who you want to become. That isn't easy. It requires you to know yourself so well that you can imagine a trajectory of your future self. And the trickiest part? Knowing where you want to go. Establishing a destination. Understanding exactly what will bring you that level of contentment in the future.

Most people have goals that are far too vague. Saying things like, "I want to make a big difference in the world," or "I want to be happy," are nearly useless. The power of a goal is in its specificity. If you not only determine where you want to go, but imagine how you'll feel when you achieve the goal, you're far more likely to accomplish it.

For others, the goal is simply incorrect. A goal that is divorced from a deeper sense of fulfillment, but is simply about externals such as, "I want to make a lot of money," will not help you. Jim Carrey is noted for saying, "I think everybody should get rich and famous and do everything they ever dreamed of so they can see that it's not the answer."[14]

In the end, people are not big chested over the wealth they've accumulated, the fame they achieved, or even the experiences they've had. At the end of life, people are most proud of who they've become.

Recently, Erica, my wife, realized her dream of becoming a full-time mom. But this, as many stay-at-home moms know, doesn't mean sleeping in until eleven and binge-watching the *Bachelorette*. Erica was intentional with her time. She set clear goals for herself and our girls.

The day after my daughter, Eden, ended kindergarten, my wife sat down with her and they made a list of the things that they wanted to do that summer. *What would make an incredible summer?* As they made the list, my wife included the typical fun summer activities, swimming, hiking, riding bikes, but she was also very careful to include challenges my daughter had yet to accomplish. Why? With three months of summer fun and relaxation ahead, Eden was ready to steer clear of anything that smelled like work. Erica wanted Eden to understand herself better at the end of summer, and she knew that identifying and overcoming weaknesses was a proven way to do it. Not only would Eden feel a sense of accomplishment as she moved into first grade, but achieving goals early in life would help Eden understand herself as someone who was capable of *becoming* someone better after just a summer of effort.

---

**TO UNDERSTAND YOURSELF, CHALLENGE YOURSELF TO BECOME SOMEONE BETTER, YEAR AFTER YEAR.**

---

If you want to understand yourself it's critical that you take on the challenge of becoming someone better, year after year. Going through the process of identifying who you want to be next year, then in five years, or ten years, or even twenty years, and then setting out to become that person will give you a deeper understanding of yourself.

If you want to become someone who takes risks, plan for it. If you want to be a more generous person, plan for that. If you want to become more self-disciplined, get in better shape, or become more creative, it's critical that you identify it and develop a vision for it.

It's incredibly difficult to develop a new vision for who you want to be while you're still in your old environment. When I try to imagine a new vision for the future, I need to surround myself with new people and new places in order to think differently. That's one reason why I jump at every opportunity to travel, or to sit down for coffee with someone who is different than I am. Simply listening to them talk about the challenges in their life or the opportunities that they are experiencing fills me with inspiration. I begin to see solutions and opportunities in my own life based on how they're leading their life.

A few years ago, I became the Executive Director of Branches Worldwide. Branches is an international non-profit that identifies and invests in emerging Christian business leaders in thirty different countries. It's a big job! And when I started, I intentionally sought out people who could help me develop a vision for my new role.

On one occasion, I drove *six* hours to Indianapolis to make a *one*-hour meeting with a man. This guy had some serious clout. He had written a popular book, traveled the world, and had served in the White House for several years. At the time he was leading a non-profit much larger than Branches Worldwide, and far too busy to meet with random people who e-mailed him. I took a risk, e-mailed him, and asked him to lunch. I think, because I was willing to drive so far to meet for a short lunch, he obliged. It was a great meeting! I learned techniques to approach donors with confidence, and how to develop relationships with leaders around the world. I learned insights I couldn't have learned in any book.

Whenever I can, I try to work with people who bring new ideas and energy to my life. My business manager, Jill, is a great example of this. When we first partnered to launch

Owolabi Leadership, I was amazed at her vision. She easily had bigger dreams than I did *and* had the drive to match it! She hit it off with my wife and kids, and I knew right away she was the type of person that I wanted to build a business with. Since we launched, we've built an incredible speaking and consulting business. By challenging me to plan further into the future, create engaging video content, and push for excellence in my interactions with clients, she's helped me become a better leader. It pays to surround yourself with people and places that make you think differently.

When it comes to understanding yourself, it's critical to author your own story, embrace your weaknesses, develop self-awareness, and create a compelling vision. A solid understanding of yourself will position you to move into the second stage of becoming an Authentic Leader—leading yourself.

**CHAPTER 7**

# Leading Yourself

## *Deliver Results*

"No discipline is enjoyable while it is
happening—it's painful! But afterward there
will be a peaceful harvest of right living
for those who are trained in this way."

People who understand themselves have an advantage, but those who have learned to lead themselves are incredibly effective leaders.

Learning to lead yourself is learning to motivate yourself, set goals for your future, create systems of accountability, and consistently follow through on promises you make to yourself. When you lead yourself, you possess self-discipline, patience, and perseverance. You've moved into the second phase of becoming an Authentic Leader. You've learned to handle the self-doubt and anxiety that comes from taking on new challenges. Deciding to lead yourself is often the first moment you'll realize your leadership potential. Only after developing new skills to overcome new challenges do many individuals believe they can lead. Those who learn to lead themselves first have the innate confidence to lead others.

## You Can't Fake Strong

About a year ago I decided to try CrossFit. I've wanted to join for years! There was something appealing about a community of people who show up at five o'clock in the morning to push each other. Everyone shows up expecting the workout to be hard, hoping that it will make them stronger than the day before. Talk about hardcore! I wanted in. Once I attended the first class I was hooked.

I was working out at CrossFit Wooster, and during a particularly sluggish workout the coach looked at our group with a disgusted "Pick up the pace!" kind of look. Then she said, "You can't fake strong."

This was a remarkably profound thing to say at 5:00 in the morning. Think about it. Strength is strength. Either you can move something with your muscles or you can't. Full stop. End of sentence. You can't pretend when it comes to CrossFit. You've either worked hard and can move the weight or you can't.

Leading yourself is similar. You can either produce results through relationships or you can't. When you're *pretending* to be a leader—pretending to be stronger, smarter, richer, healthier, a great strategist, more well connected, etc.—you *know* there's a gap between who you really are and who people think you are. Not only will insecurity grow like gangrene, but you won't be able to produce the same results as someone who can actually lead. The results of your leadership will eventually expose you.

The leader who has chosen to lead themselves is often the leader others want to follow. Deep down inside, we all want to follow leaders who have been where we want to go, where we believe it is impossible to venture without a guide. We assume they have mastered every lesson they teach.

> AUTHENTIC LEADERS ARE
> UNCOMFORTABLE SHARING LESSONS
> THEY'VE YET TO UNDERSTAND OR
> PRACTICE IN THEIR OWN LIFE.

Ray Croc, the executive most responsible for creating the McDonalds brand as we know it, understood the value of leading yourself. He said, "The quality of a leader is reflected in the standards they set for themselves." Authentic Leaders are deeply uncomfortable sharing lessons that they have yet to fully understand or practice in their own life. The most significant lessons come from their own experience. That's because Authentic Leaders know that authority derived from a position or title does not make them a leader. Rather, their influence is created when others see and respect the purpose and discipline of their day-to-day life.

## When Pretending is Valuable

Leading yourself involves the willingness to challenge yourself and push your limits. It means risking failure and trying new things. It means striving to become a better person in order to reach your potential. Paradoxically, year after year, Authentic Leaders are constantly working to become a *different* person. At first glance, this might seem like the practice of pretending and projecting that derails insecure leaders. But, it's not. Authentic Leaders are both comfortable in their own skin, while also working to be better.

The process of leading yourself always contains a process of pretending to be someone you're not. C.S. Lewis described it well.[15]

> Well, even on the human level, you know, there are two kinds of pretending. There is a bad kind, where the pretense is there instead of the real thing; as when a man pretends, he is going to help you instead of really helping you.
>
> But there is also a good kind, where the pretense leads up to the real thing. When you are not feeling particularly friendly but know you ought to be, the best thing you can do, very often, is to put on a friendly manner and behave as if you were a nicer person than you actually are. And in a few minutes, as we have all noticed, you will be really feeling friendlier than you were. Very often the only way to get a

quality in reality is to start behaving as if you had it already. That is why children's games are so important. They are always pretending to be grownups—playing soldiers, playing shop. But all the time, they are hardening their muscles and sharpening their wits so that the pretense of being grown-up helps them to grow up in earnest.

Lewis hits the nail on the head when he distinguishes when pretending is valuable: "where the pretense leads up to the real thing." You know you're on your way to Authentic Leadership when pretending and pretense are temporary. When you know that going through the motions in the present, will lead to authentic actions and emotions in the future.

Sometimes, when you act like someone you're not it's not pretending; it's practice! The best leaders understand that. They're not trying to fool people. They're actively becoming who they aspire to be.

### Growing into Leadership

Authentic Leaders don't shortcut the process of leading themselves. They understand change and growth can be a hard, slow process. They know that there are no shortcuts to becoming a better version of themselves. They know the alternative to growth is perpetual posturing and pretending.

I first learned how arduous the process of growth can be when I was thirteen.

In the seventh grade, I was introduced to track and field.

At the time, I was one of the only African Americans at Smithville's Middle School. I was tall and I hadn't yet mastered control of my gangly arms and legs. From time to time even walking felt challenging. In hindsight, making middle schoolers hurdle seems like a cruel joke by people who like watching kids suffer.

So, for many reasons, I had no interest in track. I saw myself as a basketball player. That was the identity I established. End of story.

But as track season started, one by one, people approached me to run with the team.

First, the coach. "Dan, why don't you join the track team?"

"No, I'm good," I responded.

Then it was the teachers, the principal.

"Hey Dan, why don't you consider coming out for the track team. We think you'd be great." Smile. Nod. No.

Then, a small group of students.

Female students—attractive, athletic female students— all on the track team.

"Dan, have you ever been asked to join the track team?"

"No, I haven't been asked yet. Where do I sign up?"

What I lacked in character I made up for in ... focus? Thankfully, middle-school Dan has come a long way.

I joined the track team after the season started and just one day before our first track meet. I got my jersey and race assignment before a single day of practice.

I went home filled with confidence. I remember laying on my bed dreaming about how great the next day would be. This was just the beginning! I was one day closer to breaking school records. And, do I hear a phone ringing in the distance? Are those college scouts? Mom—will you be my agent? And, I'll say yes to Nike, and maybe Pepsi, but no other endorsements.

Needless to say, the next day provided valuable lessons on earned confidence and self-leadership (and, spoiler alert, no endorsement deals). It was a no-excuses kind of day. Beautiful, seventy-five degrees, a gentle breeze. The stands were packed. The absolute perfect conditions for my debut.

When it was time for my heat to line up for the 100-meter dash, I walked confidently to the start, placed my fingers on the line, moved my gangly, giraffe legs into my stance, and waited for the gun.

I ran as fast as I possibly could. And it was textbook—for what not to do. Flailing, gangly arms, with an arched back, head tipped back, and a stride only a mother could love. I'm lucky I didn't injure myself. But I sure was working hard! Since my head was tilted back and pointed towards the sky, I didn't really see anyone in the race, or my track career ending before it started

I finished dead last.

You know those moments in your life when you expect to finish in triumph, but it ends in tragedy? That's how I felt. I was crushed.

But the meet wasn't over. And I had another opportunity to run the 200-meter dash! But, like a bad Britney Spears song, I did it again. I finished in last place.

The next day at practice coach was sympathetic. Maybe it was just the event? He suggested I try hurdles. The next meet came. And, yes, you guessed it—I finished last in that too. Hurdles were indeed my hurdle.

It gets worse.

Are you cringing yet? If not, you should be. I'm wincing just writing this.

I wasn't the only one who had high expectations for my performance. The rest of the team thought I would be the Usain Bolt of Smithville Local Schools. But once everyone learned how "talented" I actually was, the lofty expectations melted into pity.

And those beautiful, athletic recruiters? Well, I caught them mocking my form one day during practice. And so, I called it quits. My running career ended just about as soon as it began. I turned in my running jersey and any hopes of a Pepsi commercial.

When you try something for the first time and fail, it can be paralyzing. When you fail in public? Well, you can add a healthy layer of shame on top of that paralysis. An overwhelming urge wells up inside you to quit. With emotions that intense, it's nearly impossible to find reasons to put yourself through another day of misery. Walking away, you assume, will bring immediate relief and reprieve from the painful embarrassment.

I believe most leaders don't really mind losing—losing money or losing deals—just as long as they aren't publicly losing. But if you make a big mistake and the people you respect most find out? The human tendency is hang it up and walk away.

Fortunately, things didn't end when I quit the track team.

That summer my family moved from Smithville to Dalton and I started school in a brand-new district. No one knew about the tales of hurdling Dan or the newborn giraffe attempting the 200-meters. As the months at the new school passed, the sting of embarrassment at my previous school slowly dissolved. So much so that when the opportunity came to run on the track team the next year, I decided to try again.

Initially, it was very difficult. I had not improved at all from the moment I quit the year before. And that's how things tend to go. When you quit, you stop all forward progress. So, when (and if!) you pick things up, you are exactly where you left off or, dare I say, worse. But this time I decided not to quit. This time, I came early for practice and stayed late afterwards. I worried more about proper running mechanics than plaques, cute girls and Pepsi deals. Okay, I worried *as much* about proper running mechanics as I did about the plaques and cute girls. I was in middle school. What do you want from me? After several meets, shin splints, sore feet, and hours of extra practice, I still didn't win any races or break any records. But I focused on becoming better.

At the very end of the season, I had one last chance to win a race. Cue the *Chariots of Fire* music. It was at the all-county track meet. Now, at this meet every school in the county competed against each other, *including* Smithville, my old school. I still remember walking to my position for the start of the race and making eye contact with *that* group of girls from the year before.

I lined up for the 200-meter dash. The 200-meter dash runners start the race staggered around a curve. So starting in the eighth position, I could see every other runner in front of me. When the gun went off, I did the same thing I had done a year before. I ran as hard and as fast as I could, but this time, I had a season's worth of practice under my belt.

Then something surprising happened. I passed the seventh person in line, then the sixth. I can still see the bobbing head of the fifth guy. I passed him and blew past the fourth. As we left the curve and entered the straightaway, I passed the third.

At this point I could sense something special was happening and I put everything I had into the moment. With forty meters to go I passed the second person, and finally with less than ten steps to go I hurled myself across the finish line and passed the first person. I beat the best runners from every school and won the race! I may not go down in track history, but that moment went down in my history.

It was an incredible moment. It was great to win the race. But it really wasn't about winning. I came a heck of a long way from the idle daydreamer to the daily hustler. From quitting to showing up. From pretending to proving. It was then that I learned the difference between authentic confidence and artificial confidence.

The year before was artificial confidence. I had never run a race or practiced for a race. But, based on my potential, I was confident that I was going to win! Only after starting from the proverbial bottom and winning a race did I experience authentic confidence. After that moment, I held my head high. I had learned how to lead myself, and I saw a clear result from my effort. It wasn't a fluke. Every hour in practice and *after* practice led to that moment. And, I knew I could do it again. That kind of confidence becomes contagious.

> **LEAD YOURSELF, AND REALIZE YOU HAVE THE CAPACITY TO MAKE THINGS HAPPEN.**

When you learn to lead yourself, you realize you have the capacity to make things happen. That creates a deep sense of inner confidence. Show me someone who's naturally confident, and I'll show you someone who is well acquainted with long seasons of self-discipline. Those who learn to lead themselves take a more disciplined approach to life and accomplish more than most ever dream.

## Motivation from the Inside

Self-leadership always starts with an internal motivation. Authentic Leaders have an inner drive to improve. They don't need conditions to be perfect to produce results. They show up and work whether they feel like it or not. They move the needle whether people are watching or not. Sometimes leaders succeed for a short time simply because they are externally motivated. They are surrounded by an environment perfectly tailored for their success. That's a dangerous situation for a leader because they've never really been tested, but they *believe* they've learned self-discipline.

For example, *The Biggest Loser* became popular for incredible transformation of the contestants. The show documents individuals who experience extreme weight loss. Every episode involves scenes of people running, lifting, and generally pushing themselves more than they ever have. There are always moments when they cry and quit, only to get back on the treadmill again. Finally, each show culminates in a "big reveal" when the final contestant comes out from behind a curtain to reveal him- or herself. Every time, they look like a totally different person! They've lost hundreds of pounds, they've received a wardrobe makeover, and they're more confident than they've ever been. The show ends as they hug their family and friends, ready to enjoy their new life with new clothes and a new physique. It's all very inspirational.

If you follow up months later you'll see something far less inspirational. Most contestants regain the weight they lost. Some weigh *more* than when they started the show. The unfortunate reality is that their weight loss was propped up by tremendous external motivators. Imagine trying to dramatically alter your body composition. You have your entire circle of family and friends, and a bigger throng of total strangers watching your every move on national TV. Situations like that create a very compelling reason to lose weight. Add a celebrity exercise coach screaming in your ear and a cash prize at the end, and you've got a *very* strong chance of losing weight.[16]

But once the cameras stop rolling and the audience changes the channel to *The Masked Singer*, former contestants lose all external motivators. All they are left with is the internal motivation to maintain the weight loss. The secret tragedy of *The Biggest Loser* is that most people haven't developed that critical internal motivation to do it on their own. They achieved dramatic results due to the intensity of their environment instead of their ability to lead themselves. Their success was less about their internal motivation, and more about their external circumstances. If you choose to lead yourself, then by default, you are choosing to put yourself in a position where you test your internal motivation.

When a leader decides to lead themselves, it's a decision to be consistent. Your internal motivation is tested in the consistency of your actions *when no one is looking*. Setting goals, creating a plan, and finding accountability partners will help you. But there is no substitute for simply doing the work. No one can do that for you. My friend, author and speaker, John Gordon agrees. He says:[17]

> No matter what anyone says, just show up
> and do the work.
> If they praise you, show up and do the work.
> If they criticize you, show up and do the work.
> If no one ever notices you, just show up and
> do the work.
> Just keep showing up, doing the work, and
> leading the way.
> Lead with passion.
> Fuel up with optimism.
> Have faith.

Power up with love.

Maintain hope.

Be stubborn.

Fight the good fight.

Refuse to give up.

Ignore the critics.

Believe in the impossible.

Show up.

Do the work.

You'll be glad you did.

True grit leads to true success.

## Just Start

Leading yourself is about starting where you are. Instead of waiting for a day when everything makes sense (because that will be a *long* wait) and all the stars align, those who have learned to lead themselves understand that they have to make things happen when they don't feel like it. When they don't have all the information. When they don't really know what they're doing. When people don't agree. They choose to get started before they're ready. Because they know that they'll never, ever be ready. No one is.

In the Bible, there's an incredible story about a young man named Gideon. Early in the story, before he becomes a leader, he has a significant encounter with God. He's the youngest member of the smallest tribe in Israel and God calls him to lead the Israelites out of oppression, saying, "I will be with you."

Gideon has never led at the level God is asking him to lead, and he's understandably afraid. So, like you and I might do, he puts up a bit of a fight.

"Pardon me, my Lord," Gideon replied, "but if the Lord is with us, why has all this happened to us? Where are all his wonders that our ancestors told us about when they said, 'Did not the Lord bring us up out of Egypt?' But now the Lord has abandoned us and given us into the hand of Midian."

In other words, Gideon says, "I have no reason to believe this is going to turn out well. Everything in my life suggests that this will *not* end well for me—or for my people. You may want to find a sub, God."

If we're honest, we've all been there. The challenges at work, on our team, in our marriages, with our health or our finances tell us that things are not going to turn out well. While there might be risky opportunities to better our situation, it feels far safer to stay where we are, hope for the best, and wait until conditions are perfectly comfortable before we proceed.

And God says to him something we all need to hear, "Go in the strength you have … Am I not sending you?"[18]

---

**MOVE FORWARD WITHOUT EVERY COMFORT
AND ASSURANCE AND SAFETY NET.**

---

Gideon receives an incredible endorsement from God, because God essentially says, "You have enough to get started.

I'll give you what you need along the way, you simply need to start moving forward."

Deciding to lead yourself is deciding to move forward without every comfort and assurance and safety net.

- You have enough time.
- You have enough money.
- You have enough support.
- You have enough vision.
- You have enough creativity.

Leading yourself means not waiting until everything lines up, you see Ursa Minor in the sky, or the stars of Jupiter signal to you.

## The Stages of Competence

The Four Stages of Competence is a concept that's helpful when trying to understand what you'll go through when you decide to lead yourself.[19] This isn't a one-time journey. Because I continue to try new things, I constantly leave my comfort zone, put myself out there, and experience failure, I find myself returning to this diagram over and over again.

Maya Angelou is one of my favorite authors. She said, "You may encounter many defeats, but you must not be defeated. In fact, it may be necessary to encounter the defeats, so you can know who you are, what you can rise from, how you can still come out of it."[20]

Authentic Leaders understand the necessity of struggle and frustration. They know that significant growth is on the other side of significant challenges. But they don't just choose to go through difficult seasons, they choose to grow through them. The Four Stages of Competence provide a helpful roadmap for anyone attempting to learn something new. Here's how the four stages work (see Figure 2).

**Figure 2  The Four Stages of Competence**

| UNCONSCIOUS INCOMPETENCE | UNCONSCIOUS COMPETENCE |
|---|---|
| You are unaware of the skill and your lack of proficiency | Performaning the skill becomes automatic |
| CONSCIOUS INCOMPETENCE | CONSCIOUS COMPETENCE |
| You are aware of the skill but are not yet proficient | You are able to use the skill, but only with effort |

### *Stage One: Unconscious and Incompetent*

The first stage of growth starts when we think about trying something new. We are both incompetent (we have no experience) and unaware of our incompetence (we have so little experience, we think we could be *uh-mayyyzing*). Just think of "track Dan" and his Nike endorsements. When I decided to run a full marathon, I thought it was going to be easy (correct, "track Dan" got a second wind). "It's just a matter of training!" I said. By then I had run four or five half marathons and thought, "Shoot, it's just double that. I'll train a little bit harder."

I was certainly incompetent *and* (I cannot overemphasize the "and" enough) overly confident. I was blissfully unaware of how different marathon running is from any other kind of running. After the blisters, the welcoming of aching muscles I didn't even know I had, and the insatiable hunger that awaited me after every run, well, I now know. That brings us to stage two.

### Stage Two: Conscious and Incompetent

The real pain of learning anything is the second stage. This stage hit me square in the forehead during my first fifteen-mile training run. You're trying something new and now you are painfully aware just how hard it is.

This is the finding yourself in the middle of the country, not remembering the next turn for your long run, not knowing if you can put the next step forward to finish that run, and wondering what ever got in your head two months ago that suggested *this* was a good idea. This, if you haven't already surmised, is when things are most painful. You have a constant reminder that you are not living up to your own expectations. The Garmin watch. The mile pace. The sore legs. The inability to walk up or down steps. (Marathon training was challenging—have I said that yet?) If you're in the public eye, it's even worse. Your failure is exposed—to everyone. Like your training runs. (Okay, I'll stop).

This is when most people quit. This is when things take longer than expected, cost more than expected, or challenges are greater than expected. When there's a significant gap between what you expect and what you experience, people tend to quit. The best leaders have learned that this is only part of the process. Diligence, determination, and perspective can keep you focused and move past this stage.

### Stage Three: Conscious and Competent

The third stage brings noticeable improvement. It becomes a little easier to get out of bed each morning for your run. Your body doesn't ache, moan, or yell at you after five miles. Dare I say, there are times you might even enjoy getting those runs in. You have figured a few things out and you can see the trees from the forest. You know what needs to be done and you become more confident each day that you have the ability to get it done. Of course, you still need to cultivate the mental energy to stay focused as excellence is not yet a habit. And you need to remind yourself to do the small things. In other words, you're competent but need that conscious effort to make progress.

### Stage Four: Competent and Unconscious

The final stage is the destination of the best leaders. This is unconscious competence. This is the destination after years of conscious living and effort. At some point, the scales tip and you stop thinking about what you need to do—because, you already do it. It has become so engrained in your every-day life that the original effort to remember the task, stay on task, and complete the task can be moved to a new goal. In other words, you think about your morning run as much as you think about brushing your teeth. It just happens. You get out of bed, put on your running clothes, and head out the door. Like clockwork, you return.

Malcolm Gladwell's *Outliers*[21] describes this phenome-non. People become masters of the task. After so many hours of focus, your effort becomes second nature. Michael Jordan shot millions of shots before he took his first shot with the Chicago Bulls. The Beatles played thousands of hours in Liverpool before they stepped foot in the United States and became an international sensation. Martin Luther King Jr. gave hundreds of sermons and addresses before he deliv-ered his "I Have a Dream" speech. Jordan, The Beatles, and Martin Luther King Jr. are all examples of people who dis-ciplined themselves on a specific task over a long period of time and achieved levels of incredible mastery. At this stage, confidence is not contrived or projected; it's baked into who you are. It's authentic. At this stage you're not trying to run, you are a *runner.*

Some people experience confidence on a smaller scale when they learn to drive. The first time I learned to drive a standard, I was initially overconfident. (Yes, there is a pat-tern here. Yes, I am aware of said pattern.) I was dating Erica at the time and I watched her drive a stick shift car for nearly a year. Just watching her, it seemed extraordinarily simple.

From the passenger seat, there was no way to comprehend what it felt like to navigate controls with both my feet and my hand, while turning the wheel at the same time.

Then, because of an upcoming foot surgery, Erica learned that she would not be able to drive for months. Since I didn't have a car and she couldn't drive, we both needed me to learn how to drive her car. I quickly realized how much I didn't know.

I painfully progressed through that dreaded aforementioned boxes (see Figure 2). Initially I was overconfident, but as soon as I got behind the wheel in an empty parking lot, I felt the pain of conscious incompetence. The broad smile on Erica's face told me she was also conscious of my incompetence. Her smiles and suppressed snickers didn't help. I said earlier, this is the stage when people are most likely to give up.

The first time I took her car out on the road and encountered traffic was unbelievably frustrating. We were at a stop light, the first car at the intersection. The intersection quickly filled up with other cars. When the light turned green and it was my turn to move forward, I put my foot on the clutch, put the car in gear, and stepped on the gas. I wasn't halfway through the intersection when the car began to sputter and stall.

Erica was beside me, calmly giving me instructions on how to get the car moving. But I was starting to panic. By now we were stalled in the middle of the intersection, the light was still green, but *no one* was able to move because I was blocking all lanes of traffic. Then, the light turned green for the other direction. And they couldn't go forward either because I was blocking their lanes too. Simultaneously, dozens of stranded, angry drivers started honking and yelling at me. And in the Midwest, that's a huge deal. People don't honk at each other in the Midwest. It was a nightmare!

In true Dan Owolabi form, I stubbornly refused to allow Erica to take over the wheel and drive our little car to safety. As I remember it, the light turned green no fewer than three times before I finally figured out how to get the car moving. By the time I drove through the intersection, it felt like hundreds of cars were simply waiting for me to move. I'm not going to lie, I almost quit that day!

But I didn't give up. I progressed to the next stage of conscious competence. Soon I could travel to and from the store without stalling more than once or twice. And every time I got to an intersection, I had to apply extra focus to make sure I followed the mechanics and avoided the catastrophe of the previous incident.

> **LEADING YOURSELF IS A CONSCIOUS DECISION TO GO THROUGH THE FOUR STAGES OF COMPETENCE.**

Finally, one day it all clicked. I don't remember when it happened but, at some point, I stopped thinking about shifting and just shifted. I stopped worrying about stalling and just drove. I understood the mechanics of driving a standard car so well that it became second nature. Then five years after I learned to drive a standard transmission, I confidently purchased my own standard car and drove it full time.

Leading yourself is a conscious decision to go through the Four Stages of Competence. And when you struggle through each stage and emerge victorious, it will be hard to put into words just how it feels. It's those hard-fought accomplishments that you will be most proud of.

# CHAPTER 8

# Understanding Others

## *The Difference Between Power & Influence*

"The key to successful leadership
is influence, not authority."

KEN BLANCHARD

Beyond self-leadership, Authentic Leaders understand the people they lead. This is a key differentiator between leaders who simply hold a position and leaders who make a significant difference in the lives of others. It is the third stage in the evolution to being an Authentic Leader. Taking the initiative to genuinely understand other individuals will help you move beyond simply exercising power to possessing real influence.

## Power Versus Influence

Have you ever thought of the difference between power and influence? At times, they can appear similar. Here's how I define them. *Power* is the ability to get others to do your will, against their will, based on the position you have over them. *Influence*, on the other hand, can be understood as the ability to get people to do your will based on who you are, and the relationship you have with them.

I experienced the definition of power a few years ago when I was late to an important appointment. I was in my twenties, and I was flying down I-77 in my brown 2000 Honda Accord (it had a stick shift transmission, in case you were wondering) hoping to simultaneously shave some minutes off my ETA, and stay below the radar of any highway patrol officers. No such luck.

I saw the familiar flashing lights behind me as I rounded a corner.

We did the customary exchanges.

"Hello, officer."

"Good morning. Do you know why I pulled you over?"

I act confused, "Why no!"

"Oh? I was speeding? My, oh. My license and registration. Of course.

"Wait in the car."

I check the rear-view mirror. I wonder how much speeding tickets cost these days. Maybe he won't give me one? No, no. I'll definitely get one. Dang it! I see the paper. I'm getting one.

As the officer came to my window, nothing in me wanted to take the ticket. But, for some reason, I responded, "Thank you for my ticket, sir. I'm sorry I was speeding."

Now, there are two reasons I didn't speed away or argue with the officer—or do something over the top, Bonnie and Clyde style. One, my Bonnie was working and it was just Clyde. Kidding! A factor in why I didn't do it was the power of the officer's gun, which was conveniently sitting at my eye level while he spoke.

Highway patrol officers don't really make suggestions. They don't ask you to do things based on a pre-existing relationship with you. They don't know you—probably don't care to know you. They really just want you to follow the law. And, if you don't, they're in a position to write citations or make an arrest, against your will.

### Leading with Power

Most leaders operate like highway patrol officers. Their power rests on an official position or title. Being bigger, stronger, older, higher up in the organization, having more degrees, etc., often gives us opportunities to exercise authority over others. Sometimes, we confuse our power with Authentic Leadership. Telling someone what to do and influencing, motivating, and inspiring someone to do something are two very different things.

Power-based leadership has a short shelf life. People tire of barking orders, unanswered questions, mood swings, and being treated like a three-year-old, complete with "because I said so" answers. In fact, if you asked most people why they quit their last job, they'd point to a particular leader who had power *over* them, but no influence *with* them, and they got sick of it.

## POWER-BASED LEADERSHIP HAS A SHORT SHELF LIFE.

As a pastor, I've worked with scores of adults whose parents failed to understand the difference between power and influence. When I hear a man or woman say, "I knew my dad loved me, but he didn't really say it or show it," I immediately know they had a parent who struggled to apply the basic elements of building relationships in order to build influence. Instead, they exercised leadership over a family based on the fact that he or she was older or paid the bills.

Leading with power is a classic parenting blunder, and it often leads to long periods of frustration for parents and children. When children enter their teenage years, parents who have led with power quickly begin to struggle to influence their children. As a high school teacher, I observed these parents attempting to maintain authority over their rebellious teens. Eventually, many realized the ineffectiveness of power-based parenting. A teenager's free will is strong enough to oppose the power of any parent. There needs to be another way. And, there is.

### *Leading with Influence*

Influence is far more effective. As the ability to get people to do your will based on who you are and the relationship you have, influence transcends titles, age, gender, race, education, etc. It's not dependent on the external. Influence is less tangible. Influence relies on the mutual purpose and mutual respect between two people.

---

**INFLUENCE RELIES ON THE MUTUAL PURPOSE AND MUTUAL RESPECT BETWEEN TWO PEOPLE.**

---

I experienced the power of influence when I started leading in a small, deep-rooted church of about 300 people. Churches come in all shapes and sizes. This one was unique in that leadership wasn't about title as much as it was about tenure. If you were born into the church, and older than most, you automatically had influence.

As I assumed my duties as a pastor, I had a clear agenda to help grow the church and impact the community. Having attended the church for a few years before becoming a pastor, I knew my title wouldn't get me very far. I needed to develop influence. In time, I learned that the *real* leaders of the church were a small handful of elderly people. From that group, one woman emerged as the *de facto* leader of the whole bunch. Mattie Miller was her name.

A fiery woman with ironclad convictions, Mattie wasn't afraid to tell you what she thought and why you were wrong. Mattie also saw a lot of things change. In her early nineties, Mattie had several experiences with young pastors with all the ideas and energy, appearing and then disappearing after just a few years. I was twenty-five, over sixty-five years her junior. When I was born she was already 30 years older than my mom! There wasn't much I could teach her that she didn't already know.

As mentioned earlier, I'm a six-foot-four-inch, black man. Mattie's a four-foot-eleven-inch, elderly, white woman. This may come as a surprise to you, but she didn't see me as her leader.

I knew that if I was going to win over the congregation, I had to win over Mattie. But I struggled. My insecurities emerged every time I talked to her. There was normal Dan and there was anxious, self-doubting Dan. It seemed that whenever Mattie came around, anxious, self-doubting Dan would lock normal Dan in the closet. I took all her critiques personally and always came away from the conversations deflated.

These were days when a younger, more immature version of myself would have assumed that Mattie was just racist, that she'd love my ideas if my skin was a different color. Fortunately, I knew assumptions and accusations don't help in the building of relationships. Instead of doling judgment upon her, I decided to get to know her.

She loved cooking breakfast, especially ham and cheese casseroles in her home. And, theology. She loved theology. I loved breakfast! I loved theology! So, I took the bold step of inviting myself to her house. While I could have used that time to win her over to my side, to share more about why I believe what I believe (and, of course, why I was right), I didn't. I focused on Mattie, and the delicious casseroles she baked. To my surprise, she enjoyed the breakfast meeting so much that she invited me back for another one. Soon, we were eating together on a weekly basis, debating predestination versus free will, laughing over homemade ham and cheese casseroles, talking about her life history.

We met so often that one morning as I was headed out the door to see Mattie, my wife said with a smile, "Going to see your girlfriend, huh?"

I said "Yea, she's kind of cute."

Then, something incredible happened. Mattie began to open up, and I began to understand her. She described herself as one of the oldest, most conservative women in the church, which led to bouts of loneliness. Oftentimes she felt like an outsider in her own church. Young women didn't seek her out. She felt respected, but not liked. And, we all know, sometimes you just want to be liked.

She didn't have many opportunities to hold babies. She loved babies. But she rarely found opportunities to be around them. Mattie longed to just hold one. I thought about that the whole way home, and the next day I went to see Mattie with my three-month-old daughter. I told Mattie she could hold my daughter as long as she wanted. Mattie began to cry. She didn't say anything. She just smiled through tears.

Mattie and I didn't agree on everything, and there was plenty to debate. When, during our last official breakfast together, I told her I was leaving the church to start a church in my hometown, she was mad. I didn't really understand. On my last day at the church, she grabbed my wrist, looked me in the eye, and said, "You've been one of the best friends I've had in a long time." That's when I knew I had earned the right to lead Mattie. My influence went beyond my title as a pastor. She didn't care about my education, my grade point, or anything external. I had influence with Mattie because of who I was and the strength of our relationship.

How do you know that you effectively understand other people? When they believe, deep down, that you have their best interests in mind. You don't always have to like them, or their behavior, but you genuinely want the best for them. You understand what they've been through and what they need. You've learned not only to listen, but how to help them see that you're listening. Authentic Leaders take time to be with the people before leading the people.

When your only motive is to understand and serve others, you'll realize how easy it is to feel confident in your leadership. There's a time for laying out an agenda and assessing whether people are willing to follow your leadership. That's an important part of leadership… but it is *never* the first part of leadership. Authentic Leaders always attempt to build influence, before they build a following. In summary, the better you understand your team, the better equipped you'll be to lead your team, because, it will be about them—*not* about you.

## Keys to Building Authentic Influence

There are a few keys that can help you know others well and build authentic influence.

- Don't make assumptions.
- Don't jump to conclusions.
- Avoid Fundamental Attribution Error (FAE).

We all tend to make assumptions about people. While not always right, assumptions save time. For example, when I met Mattie, I had a truckload of assumptions about her habits, opinions, work ethic, willingness to change, etc. The list was wrong. I was wrong about most of them. I learned what every Authentic Leader knows: assumptions leave you at a distinct disadvantage. You think you understand the person you want to lead, but you actually have no clue. Assumptions keep leaders from doing the real and hard work to understand their potential followers.

"Jumping to conclusions" is a common negative phrase that describes a person who rushes to judgment without considering other forms of evidence. While some people have been trained and understand the whole picture and are able to do this without jumping to conclusions, the rest of us are especially susceptible to using incomplete evidence to draw inaccurate conclusions.

## AUTHENTIC LEADERS AVOID FUNDAMENTAL ATTRIBUTION ERROR.

As an Authentic Leader, it is important to avoid Fundamental Attribution Error (FAE)[22] as well. This is when a leader assumes that someone's negative behavior is due to a deficiency in their character, rather than their circumstances. Take, for example, when people show up late to a meeting. When I show up late, I know the cause is circumstance—traffic, kids, spouse, faulty alarm, etc. It is no reflection of who I am at my core. On the other hand, the people who have been waiting aren't likely to give me the benefit of the doubt. They won't consider the circumstances that made me late. They'll think I lack character and assume I must be unfocused at best, disorganized, lazy, or just plain disrespectful at worst. We're more likely to assign bad character traits to others, but blame bad circumstances for ourselves.

Leaders tend to fall for FAE more frequently because they see so many but know so few. It's easier to just assume character issues. It's really our environment, rather than our character, that is the strongest determining factor of our behavior. It's extraordinarily beneficial for leaders to get to know people as well as possible before making judgments.

### The Milgram Experiment

In the 1960s, Yale University psychologist Stanley Milgram studied the relationship between action and environment.[23] After Milgram watched the trial of WWII Nazi war criminal, Adolph Eichmann, he wondered how an individual could order the deaths of millions of Jews. Eichmann's defense? He was simply *following orders.*

Milgram couldn't get past that statement. So he developed an experiment to see if individuals, like these war criminals, were horrible human beings or human beings caught in horrible circumstances, and compelled to follow orders.

The test subjects in the experiment were average people—parents, grandparents, nurses, factory workers, and entrepreneurs—who responded to an ad that promised to pay them $4.50 for one hour of their time (an appealing hourly wage in the 1960s).

Milgram developed a shock generator that looked intimidating, with varying shock levels. The switches were labeled with phrases like "slight shock," "moderate shock," and "danger: severe shock." The last two switches were simply labeled with "XXX." This was obviously a shock most people didn't want to get.

Each test subject played the part of a "teacher." When the "student" gave an incorrect answer, the "teacher" shocked the "student." The participant believed they were delivering real shocks to the student. A "scientist" in a white lab coat oversaw the whole session, giving orders to administer shock to the students. Now, the teacher could not see the student. In fact, the student was behind a wall and knew about the experiment. The student never felt a shock, but they pretended to be shocked. Milgram's experiment was designed to test one thing—how far the test subject would go before he refused to continue to shock the student.

Throughout the experiment, the test subjects heard the students beg to be released, complain of chest pain, pound the wall, even cry. The pain, the begging, the cries only increased with each level of shock. Once the experiment went to a particular level, the students became silent and did not answer any more questions. The scientists then instructed the test subjects to treat silence as a wrong answer and deliver a further shock.

When the students' screams became increasingly intense, most test subjects anxiously asked the scientists whether they should continue. In each instance, the scientists issued a uniform series of simple, non-binding commands to encourage the teachers to continue.

1. "Please continue."
2. "The experiment requires that you continue."

3. "It is absolutely essential that you continue."
4. "You have no other choice; you must go on."

Now, let's pause for a second. If you were the teacher, at what point would you refuse to go further? You are free to leave at any time. You know where the door is. All you need to do is get up and walk away. How many average people do you think ignored the students' screams and obeyed the scientists' orders to push the "XXX" button? Milgram asked this very question of his students at Yale. They predicted three percent would deliver the maximum shock. They were wrong.

The reality? *Sixty-five percent of test subjects delivered the maximum shock!*

Only fourteen people stopped short of pushing the final "XXX" button. It's important to note that many test subjects became very uncomfortable, distraught, agitated, and angry at the scientists. However, they still followed the orders.

If you're like me, you've assumed the reason so many Nazi's participated in the murder of six million Jews was clearly on account of a deep character defect. But years after the experiment, the finding remains just as chilling. We have long made quick assumptions about why people do terrible things. That assumption proves how easy it is to make a FAE on something much more horrific than showing up late for a meeting.

Reflecting upon his experiment, Milgram famously said, "The social psychology of this century reveals a major lesson: often it is not so much the kind of person a man is as the kind of situation in which he finds himself that determines how he will act."

Now, of course, the Milgram Experiment provides a reason without providing an excuse. It doesn't clear Nazis from their actions. Even when choices are made against our better judgment, we should be held responsible for them. But it helps us to understand how powerfully conditions shape behavior. If someone is performing negatively, Authentic Leaders take time to step into their world and understand as much as they can about the situation *and* motivations that led to actions. In other words, Authentic Leadership is a contact sport.

**AUTHENTIC LEADERSHIP IS A CONTACT SPORT.**

## Mixing It Up

To lead people well, you have to get close to them, while at the same time setting boundaries. That means building a real relationship with them and engaging in the kind of constructive conflict that brings out the best in people. Let's take it step by step.

### Get Closer

Ex-FBI agent Jack Schafer outlines how to build authentic influence in his insightful book, *The Like Switch*.[24] It's essentially a process of connecting with another person without making them unnecessarily uncomfortable. There are four steps to Schafer's Friendship Formula to increase influence with others: Proximity, Frequency, Duration, and Intensity.

1. Proximity: You're in the same physical space as the person. It doesn't need to be in the same room every hour of the day, but close enough that the person can inconspicuously observe your behavior from a safe distance.
2. Frequency: You're regularly in some sort of contact with the person.
3. Duration: The length of time you spend with the person in each instance.
4. Intensity: Your ability to meet the person's emotional and/or physical needs in a given interaction.

Schafer outlined the "Golden Rule of Friendship" by saying, "If you want people to like you, make them feel good about themselves." The goal of the Friendship Formula is to create an environment where you can learn to genuinely like others, and it's easy for others to learn to like you.

For example, Authentic Leaders who have a strong influence over their teams have mastered the art of being present *with* people. Blocking out chunks of distraction-free hours with their people, they allow for unstructured, unplanned time together. They've learned how to have regular, meaningful moments with the individuals with whom they want to develop influence. They develop real relationships.

They've learned how to slowly increase the intensity of each interaction by identifying the emotional/psychological needs of the other person. Authentic Leaders take the appropriate next steps to meet that need.

Interactions with leaders who consciously (or unconsciously) follow the friendship formula produce a powerful loyalty in people. Regardless of gender, age, or racial differences, people will run through brick walls for leaders who have met at least one or two of their needs. Leaders with this kind of influence produce a particular kind of result—their children love to come home for the holidays, former colleagues call to check in, and their assistants and direct reports follow them when they leave one position to take another. They've become the leader people love to follow because they've never demanded respect. They've always earned it by intentionally building up the people around them.

On the other hand, leaders who lack proximity, frequency, intensity, duration with their people yield little authentic influence. Because, well, they're distant.

### Setting Boundaries

Most people avoid conflict. Confronting someone for their behavior is about as enjoyable as getting a tooth pulled. But, for Authentic Leaders to really earn influence with their people, they must learn how to establish boundaries and hold others accountable to those boundaries. A leader can demonstrate care for their people by creating environments where people become their best. That means saying *everything* that needs to be said with courage, compassion, and competence. If a leader fails to confront that which should be confronted, people always get hurt. Clear is kind and unclear is unkind.

When my wife was sexually assaulted, I learned that the hard way. Years ago, right before Erica and I married, she told me about a guy around town (we'll call him Will). Honestly, I didn't really believe her. She told me about how creepy he was, how he did strange things that made her feel weird. But when I asked for specifics, she couldn't really point to a clear-cut example. This being before the #metoo movement and before I had any sense of how incredibly important it was *to start by* taking women at their word, it was too easy for me to disregard it as a misunderstanding. Then, we got married. And I saw it.

## AUTHENTIC LEADERS MUST ESTABLISH BOUNDARIES AND HOLD OTHERS ACCOUNTABLE TO THOSE BOUNDARIES.

I was around her more often and, in our small town, I saw Will with her more often. It became obvious. In public, he'd give her a hug, but he'd let his hand linger on her back a little too long. Or, he'd put his hand on her shoulder and just leave it there, just long enough to catch my attention. "Erica," I confessed one day in our kitchen, "You're right. He's *definitely* a creepy guy!"

But I still didn't think it was serious enough to say anything. And it kept happening.

You know those moments when you see something, but you don't say anything the first two or three times. You know how it makes it much harder to say anything the fourth, fifth, or sixth time? That's where I was.

So, unfortunately, I continued to not say anything. My wife didn't either and (surprise, surprise) neither did Will.

Then, one day it all came to a head.

Erica and I were adult leaders in our church youth group. We were holding an overnight event and dozens of high schoolers were running around, playing football in the dark. Then one student stepped in a hole and twisted his ankle. The leaders decided to take him home. Erica and another woman volunteered to drive him.

Then, about an hour later, Erica came back. It was dark, but I could see her get out of the car and head straight for me. When she got close, I could immediately tell something was wrong. At first, she couldn't talk. Her eyes looked like she'd been crying—hard.

"What's wrong!?"

Here's what she told me.

She drove the student home. He got out and went into the house. As soon as the student entered the house, she saw another man exit the house from the side. Will. It was his house. The student was his son.

He quickly came to Erica's side of the car. Her window was down. There really wasn't anywhere she could go to get away from him. His body was blocking the door so she couldn't get out. He reached into her car, put his fingers into her hair and started stroking it, saying quietly in her ear, "Damn, you look sexy tonight."

When she told me, I was livid. I was shaking and seeing red at the same time. I told her that's not okay. "This is NOT OKAY! Someone needs to say something! He can't get away with this! He can't do that to you. He can't do that to ANYONE! Someone needs to say something!"

But no sooner had I said that, I realized the truth. That someone was *me*. All the times that I saw the smaller incidents take place, I didn't say anything. All the times that I just let it go … led to that moment. Because I didn't know how to confront with courage, compassion, and competence, I allowed the seemingly small offenses to grow into a big thing. And it led to my wife experiencing an unwelcome sexual advance. I never forgot that night. I wondered then … and I wonder today … Why didn't I call him on it before it escalated? Why didn't I hold him responsible for his actions? Why is it so hard to hold people accountable?

Here's the reality. Confrontation can be hard, so we do a whole lot of things instead of holding people accountable for their behavior.

## Lean into Conflict

Confrontation is hard, so maybe you hint and hope. This is when we're more passive; we provide small hints, saying things like "Maybe that's not the best thing." Or we make a suggestion and hope they get it. We'll give someone a look or use a particular tone. We hope they understand. We want people to know that we see what they're doing and we're not happy about it, without actually having a frank conversation about it.

Confrontation is hard. Conversations are hard. So you hope, pray, suggest the problem will solve itself. Spoiler alert—it rarely does. You assume the problem will get better over time. Somehow, at some point, they'll learn their lesson, they'll figure it out. Someone will call them out. Someone will tell them, "No!" You can be that someone.

Instead of talking about the problem or talking to someone else about the person who has the problem, you can fix the problem. You can fix the problem by talking to the person manifesting the problem. It really is that simple.

It doesn't need to be about the individual. It is, of course, about the individual's actions.

Address the actions and do so before things get worse— before they leave or quit or give up. Or worse, before you get into an argument or must confront the former problem that has now blown up.

Authentic Leaders earn influence by caring enough to hold people to a higher standard. It doesn't need to be emotional, angry yelling to insist that others change their behavior. It can be speech that's simple, clear, and firm. Again, it is about the action, not the actor.

Leaders who channel conflict to develop influence are like velvet bricks. On the outside, they appear as velvet. They're easy to talk to. They know how to care for people, pay attention to their needs. They can empathize with others. They legitimately care about you and you feel it. But inside?

They're bricks. They have clear convictions. They've done the hard work to figure out what they believe, the values they're willing to fight for. They keep their word. They're not easily swayed by popular opinions and they know how to apply consequences for inappropriate actions.

In other words, they've established standards and boundaries. Once you've done that, it is much easier to confront those who step outside of the standards and boundaries that everyone knows you've established for your people. With this approach, conflict can be incredibly constructive.

It took a difficult lesson for me to learn that. The next morning, I put those steps into practice.

Erica and I woke up with the previous night's assault fresh in our minds. At the time, we lived in a small town and I knew where Will lived. So, we got in the car and drove directly to Will's house. I knocked on the door, with Erica by my side, and when Will opened the door, I calmly looked him in the eye and spoke slowly.

"Will," I said, "I talked to Erica last night. She told me that she drove here. That you cornered her in her car. That you touched her and said things to her that were unbelievably inappropriate. She told me everything.

"Now I want to tell you something. If I ever hear that you've done that again, you'll regret it. I'll tell whoever I need to tell, and I'll do whatever I need to do to make sure it doesn't happen to Erica or any other woman again. Do you understand what I'm saying?"

Will looked at me, stumbled, nodded, and finally muttered, "Yes, I understand."

In that moment, I was acting in Erica's best interest, but I could have also been acting in Will's best interest. If he continued to act that way toward women, things were not going to end well for him. By confronting him on his behavior, in no uncertain terms, I was also doing my best to lead him toward a better path.

## AUTHENTIC LEADERS CONDITION THEMSELVES TO LEAN INTO CONFLICT.

Authentic Leaders condition themselves to lean into conflict. They've learned the value of confronting someone calmly, with courage, compassion, and competence. The result is authentic influence with the people they lead, because they've demonstrated they care enough to help others become the best version of themselves.

CHAPTER 9

# Leading Others

## *Find Your Fight*

"Every great dream begins with a dreamer.
Always remember, you have within you the
strength, the patience, and the passion to reach
for the stars to change the world."

HARRIET TUBMAN

Leaders are everywhere, but only a few understand how to authentically inspire others. These are people who have learned that inspirational leadership isn't simply about standing in front of people and giving an opinion. Instead, it's a process of discovering your own dreams, motives and fears. It's about developing authentic confidence and real, tangible skills. It's about building genuine influence and rapport with people. And once you've understood yourself, led yourself, and understood others, you are finally well positioned to inspire others to follow you.

## What's Your Higher Purpose

Every Authentic Leader has a fight, a noble cause that they're dedicated to winning. A noble cause is a challenge more difficult than you've ever tackled before. A noble cause is never about you. It's something bigger than you that requires you to grow your faith and defeat your fears.

The noble cause that grips you, and grips your imagination, is the one in which you need to rally a team around. Allow it to grip them. Let it capture their imagination. Let it be hard, challenging, and a little scary. And then call them to overcome it with you. You don't have to have all the answers; you don't have to have it planned out. You just need to have the courage to say, "This is a worthy cause and we will figure it out … but I need your help."

If you do that, remarkable things happen. The right people will say yes. They will leave their comfort zone and follow you, because you've demonstrated that you are someone who cares about them and cares about this particular vision—a challenging vision. Deep down, most people crave a clear challenge to do something great.

At the turn of the twentieth century, Ernest Shackleton embarked on a series of expeditions to the South Pole. At the time, it was an unbelievably dangerous journey that only the daring and/or stupid would make. On one particular journey, Shackleton needed more men on the expedition, so he decided to run an ad in the newspaper. How do you glamorize a difficult trip to Antarctica? If you think like Shackleton, you simply tell the truth. The recruitment advertisement for his *Endurance* expedition read like this: "Men wanted for hazardous journey. Low wages, bitter cold, long hours of complete darkness. Safe return doubtful. Honour and recognition in event of success."

> DEEP DOWN, MOST PEOPLE
> CRAVE A CLEAR CHALLENGE TO
> DO SOMETHING GREAT.

No sugar coating! And yet, almost five thousand men expressed interest. Why? Because we all want a noble cause. Everyone wants to be challenged to do something great. We know we have potential. All we need is someone we trust to grab us by the proverbial collar and ask us to be better than what we thought we could be.

## Lead by Example

In order to call someone to a challenging endeavor, you must demonstrate that you are willing to do the same. Leaders go first. Our ability to move people to action is directly proportional to their trust that we are willing to risk more than they are, that we believe in it more than they do.

A great example of this is found in the life of Mother Teresa.[25] She inspired millions of people to think about the impoverished in a new way—one that was full of compassion, rather than disdain.

Recently, I learned how Mother Teresa impacted a small town in Pennsylvania. In 1984, Scranton had a facility designed to house people with mental disabilities. By 1987 the institution was overcrowded and generally unsuitable to provide the best care for their residents. So, the board decided to create halfway houses. This would afford patients more room in the original facility, and other patients would have the opportunity to transition into the general population.

In order to build halfway houses in the city, the board needed permission from Scranton's city council. An agenda was drawn up and the meeting was scheduled. As the assembly approached, word had spread that the institution was considering building halfway houses in the city. The day of the city council meeting, hundreds of people showed up. It was standing room only. People were mad. Shouts could be heard in the crowd.

> "You will not put the halfway house in my neighborhood!"
>
> "If one of those crazies gets out and hurts my daughter …"
>
> "Why do they have to be in our city? Can't they stay where they belong?"

One by one, men and women came up to the mic and expressed outrage. They did not want people with mental disabilities in their neighborhood.

Unsurprisingly, when the issue came to a vote, the city council members unanimously voted against building halfway houses. The institution would have to find another solution somewhere else.

But no sooner had the vote been announced, than Mother Theresa appeared. Really. She walked through the back doors of city hall. She was in Scranton to receive an award and heard about the divisive issue. Having spent her life caring for the poor and marginalized, she understood the importance of this vote.

Mother Teresa walked down the center aisle to the front of the auditorium and got down on her knees. "Please, please, please, please, please in the name of Jesus," she pleaded, "make room for these children of God!" Then, she picked up her skirt, stood, and quietly walked out of the auditorium.

The silence was deafening.

The city council members looked around and asked for another vote. One by one, each member voted to build the halfway houses in their city. No one raised their voice in opposition.

How did Mother Teresa convince a room full of angry strangers to change their minds so quickly? Simply put, she walked the walk—literally and figuratively.

What always strikes me about this story is that Mother Teresa didn't have a title. She wasn't elected. She didn't really know anyone in the city, yet she had a tremendous amount of influence. She was able to call people to a higher sense of purpose. She asked people to participate in a noble cause.

Certainly, she didn't know what would happen. She didn't have plans drawn up nor a proposed budget. All she had was the testimony of her life, and the courage to call people to live a life like hers. She stood on a lifetime of suffering and sacrifice for the sake of a focused mission—care for the impoverished and marginalized—a noble cause that transcended money, safety, reputation, or power. Her noble cause wasn't about her. That's the type of noble cause necessary to pull people out of their own selfish pursuits. That's all it took to change a room full of anger into a room full of compassion.

We *expect* our leaders to have a noble cause. We expect them to refocus our priorities and help us find the courage to do the things that we would rather not do. It's the leader who has unselfishly dedicated their life to a particular fight that has the moral authority to call us to join in that fight.

## Preach What You Practice

When I actively pastored a congregation, I constantly reminded myself how important it was for me to practice what I preached. If I remained true in word and deed, I would never risk losing the congregation's confidence.

> IT'S IMPORTANT NOT TO PRACTICE WHAT YOU PREACH, BUT PREACH ONLY WHAT YOU'VE PRACTICED.

I've learned that I need to flip the script a bit. It's important not to practice what you preach, *but preach only what you've practiced.* It's critical that your actions precede your announcements. You must do something before you can say something.

Of course, it is so much easier to talk about *what needs to be done* in the company, or in the family, or on the team, but the advantage will always go to the people who simply do it. They practice it for an extended period of time, then they point to their results, saying "I can show you how to do it too."

The ability for the leader to cast vision rests on their ability to deliver results. By preaching what you have already practiced, you stand on solid ground. There will be moments when you have to call people to something that neither you nor they have ever seen before. In those moments, it's important that you don't assume the future. Instead, you simply reaffirm the values that you have practiced in the past and challenge people to carry those into the future, into a new frontier.

As you are leading others into a new venture, or better behavior, there are three things you need to have to effectively move them.

1. Grab their hearts.
2. Engage their heads.
3. Ask for their hands.

### Grab Their Hearts

Authentic Leaders take time to connect with a felt, obvious, urgent need. This often rests on your ability to use words to convey a sense of urgency. This is where the leader will affirm previously held beliefs, then challenge people to take it up a notch in service of the felt need. This is especially important when people are mired in the day-to-day grind. We need leaders to lift our eyes and our hearts and help us see what's possible on the next horizon.

### Engage Their Heads

Often, people simply need to be inspired to take on a challenging vision. But the most dedicated people need a plan. They need to see how this might unfold. What's the first step? What's the fifth step? They want to know that someone has taken the time to look at the details. It doesn't mean that plans are concrete. They simply want to know that you have done your homework. And they'll want to make it their own, so give your people an opportunity to weigh in. Engage the heart, then engage the head.

### Ask for Their Hands

This is a critical step in leading people. *Ask* them to participate. Don't *suggest*. Don't hint. Don't hope that they understand. Be explicit. Ask them to join in. Tell them exactly what meeting to go to, website to click, person to talk to, or check to write. Tell them how to do it.

I can't tell you how many people I've worked with who've had great visions, and laid out a strong plan, but when it came time to *actually asking people* to join them on the mission, they faltered. People pause at this step because this is the step that brings the possibility of rejection. When you ask people for something, they could say no. And when people say no, it can cause you to doubt your original vision.

Authentic Leaders believe in themselves and their noble cause so much that when they hear a "no" they only hear "not now." The noble cause is so real to them that they can imagine how every person who uttered "no" will eventually change their mind and ask to join the cause. Authentic Leaders believe that there are enough "yesses" out there, regardless of how many initial "nos" they hear. They just need to find them. So, they continue to ask until they have the people they need to tackle the noble cause.

# Just Be You

Authentic Leadership closes the gap between who you are and who people think you are. In other words, Authentic Leadership is being you. There's never a reason to feel insecure or fearful. You rest in the reality of who you are and what you stand for.

AUTHENTIC LEADERSHIP IS BEING YOU.

If you know who you are, the results you can produce, and you understand the people you're leading, leadership is simplified. Then, once you find a clear and compelling noble cause, you can build a tribe who will gladly help make the vision a reality. Even if they have to make drastic changes in their own lives, your influence and vision as an Authentic Leader will be compelling enough to motivate them to change. That's Authentic Leadership.

So, may you be confident in the
knowledge of who you are.
May you lead yourself before ever
attempting to lead anyone else.

May you understand the people you
lead at a deep level, serving their needs
and building genuine influence.
And may you use that influence to
pursue a noble cause and help people
reach their full potential.

# END NOTES

## Chapter 1: WHEN INSECURITY STRIKES

[1]Dave Ramsey, *The Total Money Makeover: A Proven Plan for Financial Fitness* (Nashville, Tennessee: Nelson Books, Inc., 2003).
[2]All the airline stories that follow in the next few paragraphs were found in this article: https://www.telegraph.co.uk/travel/news/ horrifying-real-announcements-made-by-pilots/

## Chapter 3: WHY WE CHOOSE INAUTHENTICTY

[3]Jerome Charyn, *Joe DiMaggio: The Long Vigil* (Yale University Press, 2011).
[4]Richard Ben Creamer's, *Joe DiMaggio: The Hero's Life* (Simon & Schuster, 2000).
[5]Billy Crystal, *Still Foolin' 'Em: Where I've Been, Where I'm Going, and Where the Hell Are My Keys*? (New York City: Henry Holt and Company, LLC, 2013), at page 167.
[6]https://qz.com/1070243/the-moment-oprah-winfrey-knew-it-was-time-to-shut-down-her-daily-tv-talk-show/

## Chapter 5: NOTHING TO HIDE, NOTHING TO PROVE, AND NOTHING TO LOSE

[7]Aaron Sorkin (creator), *The West Wing* (NBC, September 1999 – May 2006), an American serial political drama television series. This quote is taken from "The Documentary Special" that originally aired as a regular episode during season three. It celebrated the people of the real West Wing and featured interviews with

former Presidents Carter, Clinton, and Ford, Secretary of State Kissinger, and more than a dozen White House aides, chiefs of staff, and press secretaries.

[8]*Steve Jobs: Secrets of Life* (Silicon Valley Historical Assoc., 2012).

[9]https://www.cbsnews.com/news/ronald-reagan-remembered/

**Chapter 6:** UNDERSTANDING YOURSELF: TELL THE RIGHT STORY

[10]1 Sam. 17.

[11]John Maxwell, *The 21 Irrefutable Laws of Leadership: Follow Them and People Will Follow You* (Nashville, Tennessee: Thomas Nelson, 1998).

[12]Curtis Hanson (director), *8 Mile* (Universal Pictures, 2002).

[13]An organization that supports emerging business leaders with faith-based relationships and resources that give them the confidence to transform their communities.

[14]*Readers Digest*, "Quotable Quotes" (March 2006) at page 81.

**Chapter 7:** LEADING YOURSELF: DELIVER RESULTS

[15]C.S. Lewis, *Mere Christianity* (Harper Collins, 2001) at pages 187-189. (First delivered on air and then published as three books between 1942 and 1944.)

[16]See: https://www.businessinsider.com/new-show-biggest-loser-winners-regained-weight-big-fat-truth-2017-6

[17]Jon Gordon, *The Power of Positive Leadership*: *How and Why Positive Leaders Transform Teams and Organizations and Change the World* (New Jersey: John Wiley & Sons, Inc., 2017), from Chapter 11, Positive Leaders Have Grit.

[18]Judg. 6:13

[19]Management trainer Martin M. Broadwell described the model as "the four levels of teaching" in "Teaching for Learning," *The Gospel Guardian*, February 20, 1969. The model was used at Gordon Training International by its employee Noel Burch

in the 1970s; there it was called the "four stages for learning any new skill." See also: https://www.gordontraining.com/free-workplace-articles/learning-a-new-skill-is-easier-said-than-done

[20] https://www.psychologytoday.com/us/blog/the-guest-room/200902/interview-maya-angelou

[21] Malcolm Gladwell, *Outliers: The Story of Success* (Penguin Books, Ltd., 2008).

**Chapter 8:** UNDERSTANDING OTHERS: THE DIFFERENCE BETWEEN POWER & INFLUENCE

[22] The phrase was coined by Lee Ross (a professor at Stanford University and an influential social psychologist) some years after a classic experiment by Edward E. Jones (an influential American social psychologist, he is known as father of Ingratiation) and Victor Harris (1967).

[23] Milgram first described his research in a 1963 article (Stanley Milgram, "Behavioral Study of Obedience" *Journal of Abnormal and Social Psychology*. 67 (4): 371–378) and later discussed his findings in greater depth in his 1974 book (Stanley Milgram, *Obedience to Authority: An Experimental View* (HarperCollins, 1974)).

[24] Jack Schafer, Ph.D. with Marvin Karlins, Ph.D. *The Like Switch: An Ex-FBI Agent's Guide to Influencing, Attracting, and Winning People Over* (Simon & Schuster, Inc., 2015).

**Chapter 9:** LEADING OTHERS: FIND YOUR FIGHT

[25] Mother Teresa (1910–1997) was a Roman Catholic nun who devoted her life to serving the poor and destitute around the world. She founded the Missionaries of Charity in Calcutta, India, was awarded the Nobel Peace Prize in 1979, and was canonized as Saint Teresa in 2016.

# ABOUT THE AUTHOR

Dan Owolabi has always believed that the greatest leaders are servants first. That's why he has made it his mission to help others achieve exceptional results by leading from a mindset of serving.

Drawing upon his talent for storytelling and his passion for connecting with others, Dan has spent the past 15 years working to empower those around him. For nearly a decade, he served as a public school teacher and pastor in Northeast Ohio. The work, while demanding, was incredibly rewarding—so in 2017, Dan decided to take his passion for developing leaders to a wider audience.

His immediate success and subsequent speaking invitations eventually led Dan to start a company dedicated to training and inspiring leaders around the country. By guiding them to build stronger relationships, he has been able to share his fiercely held principle that leadership isn't a status you get, but a service you give.

Now, Dan continues using his expertise to inspire fellow leaders on a global scale as well as within his own community. In 2018, he also accepted the executive director position at Branches Worldwide, an innovative non-profit aiming to impact 30 leaders in 30 countries for 30 years.

Throughout it all, Dan remains committed to looking inward as well as outward, continually pushing himself to embody the beliefs he so passionately shares with others. And while he has helped thousands of business executives, educators, athletes, and young adults to lead more effectively, he is the first to recognize that his own most important leadership responsibility remains to his wife Erica and their two daughters.

Dan holds an undergraduate degree from Malone University and a graduate degree from Ashland University. When he isn't traveling or speaking, he is most often reading, running, and spending time with his family.

# LEAD AS YOUR MOST AUTHENTIC SELF

**For more information about Executive Coaching, Keynote Speaking, or for general questions visit:**

owolabileadership.com

Owolabi Leadership

Dan Owolabi